Culture as Politics

Culture as Politics

Selected Writings of
Christopher Caudwell

Edited by
David Margolies

PLUTO  PRESS

First published 2018 by Pluto Press
345 Archway Road, London N6 5AA

www.plutobooks.com

British Library Cataloguing in Publication Data
A catalogue record for this book is available from the British Library

ISBN   978 0 7453 3723 4   Hardback
ISBN   978 0 7453 3722 7   Paperback
ISBN   978 1 7868 0175 3   PDF eBook
ISBN   978 1 7868 0177 7   Kindle eBook
ISBN   978 1 7868 0176 0   EPUB eBook

Typeset by Stanford DTP Services, Northampton, England

Simultaneously printed in the United Kingdom and United States

Contents

Introduction

Christopher Caudwell died in defence of the Spanish Republic, covering the retreat of his company in the Battle of Jarama. He was only 29 when he died, yet he had already published five books on aeronautics and seven works of crime fiction under his real name of Sprigg, and his most important work, *Illusion and Reality*, written under the pen-name of Caudwell, was in press when he died. *Illusion and Reality* and the essays subsequently published as *Studies in a Dying Culture* were widely read and admired during the war and in the post-war spirit of democracy. For people concerned with creating a fairer, better world Caudwell's work had strong appeal. He saw the problems of the world not as inherent in the human condition but as susceptible to change, and his prose had an attractive energy and optimism. Today, amidst increasing corporate dominance of everything, unstable democracy and rising right-wing populism, Caudwell's analyses show not only how culture is shaped by the social-economic structure of the time but also how it is important in shaping public attitudes. His explanations make sense at the level of human experience.

Caudwell was an autodidact. He left school at 15 and gained a wide knowledge of science and literature on his own. When he left school, he moved with his journalist father, whose career was in decline, from London to Bradford. His father took up a position as literary editor on the *Yorkshire Observer* and Christopher himself started work as a cub reporter on the same paper and also wrote occasional book reviews. Father and son led an unsettled existence in boarding houses, which is reflected in some of Caudwell's best short fiction; one of his stories suggests that he secured his own space by constantly retreating into a book. In 1925, he returned to London to join his brother in aeronautical publishing. The choice may seem strange for someone so orientated to literary culture and who considered himself a poet, but it was not accidental – both brothers had a strong interest in engineering and technical innovation and aircraft still had the excitement of a pioneering industry. As well as writing technical reviews, Christopher gained his own pilot's licence and wrote five books on flying. For him, flying was never just a means of transportation – there was a thrill in flying: 'There is nothing in the world like being in complete charge of that responsive creature, an aeroplane, with all the air in front of you, and confidence in your power to make it obey your will,' he wrote in *Let's Learn to Fly!* (*LLF!*).[1] The crime novel considered by some specialists to be his best is set in a flying club and conveys the attraction of flying. Aircraft design and production involved the most advanced engineering of the day; he was exploring new territory – 'behind it all is the thrill of mastery of man's latest and most difficult conquest, the ocean of air' (*LLF!*, p. 209). There was adventure in flying: 'The older pilots … are the real heroes of the air,' he wrote, 'although one hears little about their work. They faced all the dangers of early commercial aviation in the 1920s, in rickety, temperamental aeroplanes, with uncertain engines, and almost no ground organization. It is their splendid tradition that is inherited by the younger pilots who follow them …' (*LLF!*, p. 208). It is probably this appreciation of testing the limits of machine and man that accounts for his friendship with Clem Beckett, his partner on the machine gun at which they both died. Beckett was a national hero of motorbike racing, someone who had been cheered by crowds across European circuits, whose appearances were well paid but who had also organised the exploited speedway riders into a union.[2] The close relationship between the intellectual and the daredevil racer may seem improbable but both had chosen – one at the height of his fame, the other on the verge of recognition – to risk their lives to fight fascism; they shared a strong attraction to speed, they wanted to know how things worked and they admired courage.

Caudwell's orientation towards practical matters is of central importance to his theoretical work. He was concerned more with the concrete explanations of how things functioned, than with their philosophical implications. Aeronautics is an obvious aspect of this, as is the article he published in *Automobile Engineer* in 1929 – 'Automatic Gears: The Function of the Moving Fulcrum in Determining Design'. But he was also intensely occupied with psychology, with anthropology and sociology, and with the economic organisation of society – with how things worked on a larger scale. His involvement with crime writing began when he said that anyone could write a crime novel overnight and was given the challenge of writing one in a fortnight – which he did, and went on to write six more. Crime fiction is a part of his concern with practice; for him it was not simply a matter of ingenious clues and making the pieces fit together, but how the psychology of individuals functioned in a social context. He was very successful as a crime writer and most of his books were published by an American crime fiction club. The books gave him a platform for incidental social comment. In the earliest, *Crime in Kensington* (1933), he positions his characters to make a comment on the narrowness of a justice system that ignores the context of the crime. The killer, an older woman who has killed two people who have been blackmailing her daughter, decides not to kill a woman who could expose the daughter, on the condition she does not reveal the information. The victim, about to be released, reflects on her captor: 'she was not fundamentally a killer, but a harassed mother with the atavistic fixity of purpose of a less squeamish age.'[3] *Fatality in Fleet Street*, also from 1933, deals with the murder of a bully, a war-mongering press baron.

This My Hand (1936) he regarded as a 'serious' novel and signed it Caudwell (his mother's maiden name) rather than Sprigg because he joked he couldn't risk losing his credibility as a crime writer. The novel received praise as a brilliant psychological case study; unfortunately, it reads rather like a case study. The characters are usually presented in an external analytic perspective without much dialogue that would individualise them, and the writing lacks the light, stylish tone that gives personality to his crime fiction. However, throughout there is a strong sense of class injustice and the conclusion makes a moving argument against capital punishment through the responses of the condemned hero, the prison staff and the governor.

Caudwell's crime fiction undercut conventional views of colonialism, empire, class and gender. Unusually for the time, he also displays a proto-feminism in all his fiction. Women in his crime novels are given demanding roles and never are merely objects of masculine interest; they are shown to be the equals of, and sometimes superior to, the men they have to deal with. Thus in *Death of an Airman* (1934), the heroic figure, a female drug-runner, is a skilled pilot, intelligent and courageous. In *The Corpse with the Sunburnt Face* (1935), Caudwell mocks the misjudgements made by the vicar of the Berkshire village of Little Whippering, which are based on the racist and sexist assumptions common in his parish. In his first flying instruction book – though his nominal co-author, Capt. H. D. Davis AFC, wrote a classically sexist introduction: '... a really good or reliable woman pilot is extremely rare. Most of those who passed their tests seem thereafter to alternate between a sort of blindness, unconscious recklessness and a tendency to lose their heads'[4] – Caudwell does not draw gender distinctions in regard to flying and, as his *Death of an Airman* shows, he believes women can be as competent pilots as men.

CAUDWELL AND MARXISM

Despite his curtailed formal education, Caudwell was certainly an intellectual, and the fact of his self-education had some advantages. He was less exposed to the indoctrination suffered by people who go through the educational system, whose learning takes place in a context of received ideology, of shared assumptions about the world. He was freed to form his ideas and make his intellectual connections without pressure to conform. This is not to deny that there would have been things to be gained from more formal education, nor to claim that he remained completely unaffected by the dominant ideology; but because he was outside the confines of institutional learning, he would have escaped much encouragement to conform his thinking to the received patterns of the day. Caudwell's ability to look at the world in a different way proved a great strength; and, coupled with his interest in how things actually work, it enabled extraordinarily creative thinking.

Caudwell's coming to Marxism was an important step in his creative vision. In 1934, during a period of social deprivation and unemployment, of rising fascism and military expansion, Marxism's view that capitalism will destroy itself must have made obvious sense. But Marxism probably also attracted Caudwell because of his desire to understand how things worked. He realised that capitalism, as an economic system, had inherent design faults: it failed not because of individual greed or because its objective was to create personal wealth, but because its fundamental principles produced the opposite of what they were intended to produce. Unemployment, misery and war were not supposed to be features of capitalism. Marxism gave him the key to this complex of contradictions. It provided a unified vision of the social system and also, of obvious importance to Caudwell the poet, a guide to understanding the place of poetry in society. In the introduction to *Illusion and Reality* (*IR*), he wrote, 'There is only one sound sociology which lays bare the general active relation of the ideological products of society with each other and with concrete living – historical materialism. Historical materialism is therefore the basis of this study.'[5] His intended subject was the historical development of English poetry and his intended method was historical materialism, that is, Marxist examination of historical development in relation to the economic structure of society.

But simply to say that Caudwell was a Marxist, when the term covers such a diversity of intellectual behaviour, is insufficient. Many people's acquaintance with Marxism comes from university courses that treat Marxism abstractly as a philosophy but neglect what Marx himself considered its essential element: practice. One of Marx's best-known statements is his eleventh Thesis on Feuerbach: 'Philosophers have only *interpreted* the world in various ways; the point, however, is to *change* it.' Caudwell accepted this as a call to action, as did many others, but, unusually, he also adopted it as a principle of analysis. He looked at social processes in terms of their relation to change – the nature of mankind was to deal with the world in an active way, to change things. Caudwell's experience in aeronautics and his productivity as a writer meant that making and doing had a fundamental place in his thinking, and his focus on poetry in *Illusion and Reality* emphasised its relationship to material life. 'Poetry is what happens when it is read,' he said, a distillation of his active view. He saw that concreteness and social practice were fundamental to the development of Marx's thinking: 'the understanding of concrete living came to appear to Marx as primary to the understanding of the products of concrete living' (*IR*, p. 15). That is, if you wanted to understand what people made and did, if you wanted to understand their poetry, Caudwell, following Marx, said you had to understand how they lived. Of course, people's thinking was individual – but only to a degree; in shared social conditions that shaped thought the focus shifted from individuals to class.

For Marx, class was a central point in this understanding:

In the social production of their means of existence men enter into definite, necessary relations which are independent of their will, productive relationships which correspond to a definite stage of development of their material productive forces. The aggregate of these productive relationships constitutes the economic structure of society, the real basis on which a juridical and political superstructure arises, and to which definite forms of social consciousness correspond. The mode of production of the material means of existence conditions the whole process of social, political and intellectual life. It is not the consciousness of men that determines their existence, but, on the contrary, it is their social existence that determines their consciousness.[6]

For Caudwell this meant that poetry had to be understood in terms of class as well as individual motives. In his paraphrase, he extracts a simple, experiential notion of class:

> For a class, in the Marxian sense, is simply a group of men whose life-experiences are substantially similar, that is, with less internal differences on the average than they have external differences from the life-experiences of men in other classes. This difference of course has an economic basis, a material cause arising from the inevitable conditions of economic production. Therefore the artist will necessarily integrate the new experience and voice the consciousness of that group whose experience in general resembles his own – his own class. (*IR*, p. 226)

Caudwell saw that literature has a function in sharing consciousness and transmitting class values. In terms of conventional literary studies, this is obviously revolutionary: not only does he move away from the habit of literature courses which focus on the individual works and treat them as independent, he also presents literature as having a practical function. Again, 'the point is to change it.'

Caudwell takes a similar position in regard to language, rejecting the philosophical position that language exists simply to assert facts. He says that language does not only present information: 'The business of language, as an extension of life, is to decide what facts are worth asserting or denying ...' (*IR*, p. 218). As a product of social activity, of people doing things, language necessarily acquires an emotional content:

> It is precisely because language expresses feeling, is a judging as well as a picturing of parts of reality, that it is valuable. Language expresses not merely what reality is (what reality is stares man in the face) it expresses also what can be done with reality – its inner hidden laws, and what man wants to do with it – his own unconscious necessities. Language is a tool to express what reality is in relation to man – not abstract man but concrete human beings. (*IR*, p. 219)

Language, too, is part of changing the world. Intellectual production is rooted in practice, and its purpose and development are tied to activity in the material world.

FROM 'VERSE AND MATHEMATICS' TO *ILLUSION AND REALITY*

In relation to his writing, Caudwell's commitment to Marxism was already present when he was working on the predecessor of *Illusion and Reality*, 'Verse and Mathematics', an extensive study (unfinished and unpublished) of the balance of emotion and rationality in different intellectual fields, psychology and imagination. The study provided a basis for *Illusion and Reality* but was transformed analytically and politically by his developing Marxist orientation. (The residue of 'Verse and Mathematics' is seen most obviously in the analysis of the formal characteristics of poetry and of the relation between science and art, sections which are less integrated into Caudwell's developing sense of literature as action, are less original and are less relevant to our contemporary concerns and therefore have not been included in this volume.) A more immediate stimulus for the directional shift from 'Verse and Mathematics' to *Illusion and Reality* was an article by C. Day Lewis in *Left Review* of July 1935, 'Revolutionaries and Poetry'. Day Lewis argues that writing poetry is not just satisfaction of personal desire but has a social role: 'For centuries before this poetry represented the clearest insight into reality possible to mankind, and the poet was honoured as the spokesman of his social group and he expressed what they were feeling both as a group and as individuals.[7]

This accounts for poetry's value as historical evidence, 'even if it had not been underlined by Marx and Lenin ... It discloses for us emotionally, as science does intellectually, the hidden links in nature' (*IR*, pp. 51–2). Although he makes clear that poetry is not propaganda, it still has a social effect; in its personal quality, poetry lodges in the reader's emotions:

Poetry was a necessary activity of primitive life. We still find the most vivid, poetical use of language amongst peasants. Now these emotions, based on the fear of cold and hunger, are as keen to-day as they were ten thousand years ago: they have grown a little more complex through the increased complexity of economic conditions: but their sources are the same. Poetry was one of the chief instruments through which primitive man, by expressing his emotions, gained strength to fight against the economic conditions which gave rise to those emotions. It is bound up therefore with our emotional life, and there seems no reason to suppose that it is less necessary to us than it was to our early ancestors. (*IR*, p. 56)

Day Lewis's article was short, only six pages, but it provided the perspective that Caudwell needed to anchor his own argument: poetry gives people the emotional strength to deal with, and change, their reality. And, of course, as the reality changes, so will the poetry needed to deal with it.

With what he learned from Marx and the focus supplied by C. Day Lewis, Caudwell developed his theory of function, that literature was not merely a reflection of the world in which it was created; it was also an imaginary transformation of that world – an 'illusion' that gave an emotional impulse to making change. The theory was revolutionary and thoroughly Marxist. But even though as he believed poetry, through most of human history, had been an important tool in focusing social attitudes, by the mid-1930s the audience for poetry had become too small and certainly too specialised for it to be an effective agent of change. There is no reason to dispute that conclusion, but poetic composition was not the only form of creating the 'illusion' that could help change the world. Cinema was recognised by Lenin and by Mussolini as exceptionally important social tools of the modern age; Caudwell neglected it. His justification could have been that, as the sub-title indicates, *Illusion and Reality* is about the sources of poetry. Fortunately, the principles he advanced for poetry apply at a general level to most of the arts, and, except for specific poetic techniques, are as helpful for understanding cinema as for poetry.

PROBLEMS OF RAPID DEVELOPMENT

Caudwell was a phenomenally fast writer. Much of this can be attributed to his work as a journalist where he managed several writing jobs at once. He edited and wrote under various pseudonyms articles in *British Malaya*, the journal of the Association for British Malaya. Working with his brother in their firm Airways Publications, he edited or wrote for the magazines *Airways* and *Aircraft Engineering*, and for *Who's Who in Aviation*, at the same time as writing his books on aeronautics. We know he managed his first crime novel in a fortnight and while he was working on 'Verse and Mathematics', he wrote to a friend, 'The ideas have been pouring out at the rate of 4–5000 words a day![8] But his *thinking* had been developing over a long time. He wrote to his brother, 'I have had bits of it in my mind for a long time. It incorporates all the biological, psychological, etc. etc., theories I have been forming in the course of my reading during the last few years.' Although the ideas were in gestation over a number of years, the writing was accomplished in little over a year. The speed of composition was extraordinary – he told his brother he was averaging 4,000 words a day, not counting his bread-and-butter writing. It is unlikely that much revision could take place under such conditions, which helps to explain why the expression is sometimes unclear and he is occasionally repetitive.

Caudwell also uses a lot of specialist expression drawn from his reading in different fields which he doesn't explain (this is more frequent in the chapters of *Illusion and Reality* not selected for this volume). Some terms are unclear simply because they are long outmoded (Caudwell died in 1937; much of his reading would of course have been written a good while earlier). But it is possible that his employment of a battery of semi-scientific terms was also a defensive measure. That is, Caudwell – as an autodidact, commercial writer and 'writer of low-brow detective tales' (his term) – might have expected to be seen an unlikely author of an important theoretical tome, and in such a situation it is understandable that he might have had some uneasiness about his book's reception. He described the work in a letter to his brother, in his usual facetious style, as 'a super-technical copper bottomed piece of literary criticism, too frightfully fundamental, very revolutionary and disgustingly erudite'. In another letter to friends, he wrote that he had given *Illusion and Reality* 'a very impressive bibliography of 200 or 300 learned books I have drawn on (intended chiefly to strike terror in the heart of the reviewer!)'.

There is also in Caudwell's work a problem with major terms that shifted in his writing, especially 'bourgeois' and 'illusion'. Thus he writes that England is the paradigmatic bourgeois society: 'It is no accident that this same country, England, has also been notable for the volume and variety of its contribution to modern poetry' (*IR*, p. 66). The early use of 'bourgeois' in *Illusion and Reality* refers to a forward-looking class, transforming society in a positive way. Initially, it seems that it will benefit all individuals, freeing them from the restrictions of feudalism, but when capitalism, the bourgeois economic structure, ceases to develop, it becomes a brake on society and produces the opposite of what it intends, not freedom but wage-slavery, waste, slumps, depressions and war. By the time he is writing the essays of *Studies*, 'bourgeois' no longer conjures up the picture of a class thrusting its way to freedom but the opposite: a class with an ideology of individualism that blocks the possibility of achieving the very freedom it is supposedly advocating. It is obviously the same class but in a different context different aspects have become more important for Caudwell.

The change of Caudwell's use of 'illusion' can be better understood in reference to the change of value he attaches to 'bourgeois'. When he explains the functioning of poetry in a pre-industrial context, 'illusion' is a vision, a fantasy, something that is not a material reality. He uses it as a quasi-technical neutral term that has to do with the mental state accompanying the tribal, pre-industrial poetry-music-dance experience – a hyper-reality. However, when he moves to his own period, the focus switches from the form to the content; i.e., 'illusion' is still a vision but now what it envisions is false. Thus it acquires a negative meaning – 'illusory'. It is still immaterial and fantasy but misleading – more 'delusion' than simply 'illusion'. This confusion led the German translator of *Illusion and Reality* to add *Bürgerliche* (bourgeois) to 'illusion' in the title. This misses Caudwell's point, of course, that the poetic illusion has a general function – it is not tied to bourgeois consciousness – it can be a vision that helps to create the consciousness and unity that not only offers a picture of reality which is shared and common, but helps to make it deliverable. It helps to realise – i.e., make real – the 'reality' in the vision. It is that process of an emotionally charged vision directed toward reality that he sees as the general function of poetry. Two other terms might create some confusion – 'dialectics' and 'determined'. 'Dialectics' has become mystified, a term with magic resonance but with unclear application. Caudwell uses dialectics to convey studying things in movement and in context. Motion or change is the natural state of things and in actual life there is always context. Dialectics sees the interaction of things that are bound together in such a way that a change in one of the elements necessarily involves change or re-positioning in the other elements and therefore in fact in the whole configuration. At the simplest level, in the abstract, dialectics concerns the relation between front and back, or inside and outside, etc. When the subject involves humans, instead of an abstraction, the variables will be greater and the matter therefore significantly more complex. And if there is a macro-scale subject (society or the economic system), the variables are massively increased, are less stable, change at different speeds and move in different directions. The whole becomes extremely complex. This is why economic forecasting, for example, is considered to have so little chance of being accurate in a real world. But there is in popular media a habit of abstraction, of reducing the number of real factors or freezing their movement into a snapshot. This simplification is a falsification. The real world is in constant change – and this is what dialectics addresses.

Caudwell showed a dialectical turn of mind long before he came to Marxism. His invention of an automatic gear based on a moving fulcrum illustrates this. Most people probably learned something about the theory of fulcrums in primary school maths or science and, at a practical level, understood fulcrums through, for example, the see-saw. In regard to the see-saw, the problem of balance is not complex because there are few components and also because the fulcrum does not move and thus the only variables are the weights and the distance from the fulcrum. However, it is easy to imagine that, if the fulcrum were moving, the problem would be complex. Seeing dialectics in material terms does not make it less complex but it removes the mysticism.

The popular prejudice that 'determinism' denies the possibility of free will is, for Caudwell, a species of mystification. It is effectively denying the possibility of control by making mysterious things that are potentially explicable. At various points, he argues against religious mystification – faith is essentially mystical because it rejects the role of evidence – but his rationalist concern is more with an anti-scientific attitude. Cause and effect are an aspect of the material world. Every effect has a cause, and to designate an effect as 'random' or 'accidental' means only that the cause is not yet specified. There are no uncaused effects; an effect results *necessarily* from a cause. If we understand causation, then some choice of effects is possible. But if we reject cause and effect, then we cannot make a meaningful choice. Science and rationality are determinist. Caudwell's view is clear in *Illusion and Reality*'s epigraph, taken from Engels: 'Freedom is the recognition of necessity.'

THE ORDER OF COMPOSITION

We know from his letters that Caudwell wrote *Illusion and Reality* first and wrote the essays of *Studies in a Dying Culture* shortly after, just before leaving for Spain. *Illusion and Reality* is, however, theoretically more advanced although *Studies* is more orderly and seems more finished. The explanation, I think, lies in Caudwell addressing two different sets of demands. Through most of *Illusion and Reality* he is explaining his theory of the function of the arts but in the final chapter, where he deals with the present, he changes his tone and direction – he moves further into political persuasion. He had been living happily with his brother and sister-in-law in Surrey, in the London commuter belt but then moved to the working-class east London district of Poplar and joined the Communist Party. He lived in a house with other comrades and shared party tasks such as selling the *Daily Worker*. He had become an activist and his life was now organised in terms of political struggle.

'The Future of Poetry', the final chapter of *Illusion and Reality,* praises the Soviet Union as the model of the post-capitalist society of the future. Caudwell also points out that artists and professional intellectuals in all disciplines are allying themselves with the proletariat in the People's Front, an umbrella organisation of anti-fascists. The chapter fulfils political duty but suffers from rather forced arguments about Soviet democracy and what writers must do as writers to meet their political responsibilities. Caudwell constructs a speech addressed to 'all bourgeois revolutionaries' and spoken by 'the conscious proletariat'. The logic of the demand to accept proletarian discipline is a bit abstract but the change in the form of presentation of the argument is striking and significant: it is highly unusual that in non-fiction he should speak through the voice of a character; its awkwardness suggests some difficulty with the argument. The conclusion of the address says: 'You are not now "just an artist" (which means in fact a bourgeois artist); you have become a proletarian artist' (*IR*, p. 319). Although he sees what has to be done in the art world, he also sees that the artists are 'not fit for purpose' – he is caught in an impossible position. For poetry, the time is out of joint: the poet cannot be the leader of revolution 'because his world has become by the pressure of alien values too small a part of the real world and it is part of the task of the revolution to widen it' (*IR*, p. 326).

Caudwell's analysis of the way the development of economic structures has shaped cultural production and the functional role of the arts is indeed revolutionary, but it was clear in his last chapter of *Illusion and Reality* that he had already recognised that the rise of fascism made demands of a different order. The problem now was immediate and demanded a more direct style. In *Studies* he refocuses, assuming a more militant posture and making better use of his journalistic skills. The essays deal with what is wrong with bourgeois culture in the present. They have a better pace than *Illusion and Reality* and their statement is sharper and clearer. Caudwell is also more attuned here to other people's ways of looking at things; he realises his task is not just to construct an argument that can be persuasive but actually to persuade, to persuade people who may well see the world in quite a different way. His theories as a critic have at this point led him to a different practice. The energy of the essays in *Studies* comes across well; this is vigorous argument that makes them attractive to read. It should not be surprising that in the current crisis-riven period they remain relevant.

PART I

Studies in a Dying Culture

Studies in a Dying Culture was published by The Bodley Head in 1938 and was reprinted five times in the decade after the war. It was Caudwell's most accessible theoretical work and probably the most popular at the time. Whereas *Illusion and Reality* can seem rather formidable, with a bibliography that Caudwell jokingly said was designed to terrify reviewers, *Studies* contains more clearly focused essays which are fairly short and must seem more manageable. The topics had a more obvious relevance than the 'study of the sources of poetry' which the subtitle of *Illusion and Reality* suggested.

The essays of *Studies* were radical, explicitly so, and the subjects were examined against a political background. The rise of fascism and the growing resistance from the Popular Front – the People's Front as it was in Britain – made the issues sharper. Writers as citizens and as writers had to take sides; Writers' International allied itself to 'the class that will build socialism'. Caudwell's joining the International Brigades to fight fascism confirmed his citizen commitment; *Studies* is a clear demonstration of his commitment as a writer.

The effect of writing from commitment meant that the balance of explanation and argument shifted; the essays were propagandistic in their advocacy. They are more tendentious than his writing that is not shaped to a political purpose, but what they lose in nuance they gain in rhetorical vigour. They have a tremendous energy, which sometimes overruns their logic. In evaluating Freud's contribution to human understanding, for example, Caudwell's conclusions have a good balance but he commits occasional excesses in passing which he then modifies, for example, 'Freudism, attempting to cure civilisation of its instinctive distortions, points the way to Nazism.' Freud, he says explicitly, rejects fascism but promotes a bourgeois misunderstanding of the nature of society which can point to fascism.

Similarly, Caudwell says of D. H. Lawrence, 'it is Lawrence's final tragedy that his solution was ultimately Fascist and not Communist' because he is advocating a return to the primitive (he is not taking up fascist politics). The point for Caudwell is that Lawrence's reaction to the decline of human relations is backward-looking: he refuses to understand that society is what makes humans human, whereas a blind retreat into the body in fact negates the very thing that transforms the beast into the human. This essay is Caudwell's most eloquent plea to recognise the fundamental role society plays for humanity.

The final essay of the book, 'Liberty', is one of Caudwell's most thoroughly developed arguments. Again, he is insistent about the fundamental role of society, without which liberty is meaningless. Politically, it is one of the most important pieces of his writing, not because of party advocacy, but because it examines views about freedom that are important in making political choices, are commonly held throughout bourgeois culture and are fundamentally wrong.

These three essays are, I think, the most relevant of the collection and best stand the course of time. They are presented in the order in which they appear in the original volume. The essays I have not included were on George Bernard Shaw, T. E. Lawrence, H. G. Wells, Pacifism and Violence, and Love.

The appearance of * * * in the essays indicates text that has been left out of this edition.

1

D. H. Lawrence:
A Study of the Bourgeois Artist

What is the function of the artist? Any artist such as Lawrence, who aims to be 'more than' an artist, necessarily raises this question. It is supposed to be the teaching of Marxism that art for art's sake is an illusion and that art must be propaganda. This is, however, making the usual bourgeois simplification of a complex matter.

Art is a social function. This is not a Marxist demand, but arises from the very way in which art forms are defined. Only those things are recognised as art forms which have a conscious social function. The phantasies of a dreamer are not art. They only become art when they are given music, forms or words, when they are clothed in socially recognised symbols, and of course in the process there is a modification. The phantasies are modified by the social dress; the language as a whole acquires new associations and context. No chance sounds constitute music, but sounds selected from a socially recognised scale and played on socially developed instruments.

It is not for Marxism therefore to demand that art play a social function or to attack the conception of 'art for art's sake' for art only *is* art, and recognisable as such, in so far as it plays a social function. What is of importance to art, Marxism and society is the question: *What social function is art playing?* This in turn depends on the type of society in which it is secreted.

In bourgeois society social relations are denied in the form of relations between men, and take the form of a relation between man and a thing, a property relation, which, because it is a dominating relation, is believed to make man free. But this is an illusion. The property relation is only a disguise for relations which now become unconscious and therefore anarchic but are still between man and man and in particular between exploiter and exploited.

The artist in bourgeois culture is asked to do the same thing. He is asked to regard the art work as a finished commodity and the process of art as a relation between himself and the work, which then disappears into the market. There is a further relation between the art work and the buyer, but with this he can hardly be immediately concerned. The whole pressure of bourgeois society is to make him regard the art work as hypostatised and his relation to it as primarily that of a producer for the market.

This will have two results:

(i) The mere fact that he has to earn his living by the sale of the concrete hypostatised entity as a property right – copyright, picture, statue – may drive him to estimate his work as an artist by the market chances which produce a high total return for these property rights. This leads to the commercialisation or vulgarisation of art.

(ii) But art is not in any case a relation to a thing, it is a relation between men, between artist and audience, and the art work is only like a machine which they must both grasp as part of the process. The commercialisation of art may revolt the sincere artist, but the tragedy is that he revolts against it still within the limitations of bourgeois culture. He attempts to forget the market completely and concentrate on his relation to the art work, which now becomes still further hypostatised as an entity-in-itself. Because the art work is now completely an end-in-itself, and even the market is forgotten, the art process becomes an extremely individualistic relation. The social values inherent in the art form, such as syntax, tradition, rules, technique, form, accepted tonal scale, now seem to have little value, for the art work more and more exists for the individual alone. The art work is necessarily always the product of a tension between old conscious social formulations – the art 'form' – and new individual experience made conscious – the art 'content' or the artist's 'message'. This is the synthesis, the specifically hard task of creation. But the hypostatisation of the art work as the goal makes old conscious social formulations less and less important, and individual experience more and more dominating. As a result art becomes more and more formless, personal, and individualistic, culminating in Dadaism, surréalism and 'Steining'.

Thus bourgeois art disintegrates under the tension of two forces, both arising from the same feature of bourgeois culture. On the one hand there is production for the market – vulgarisation, commercialisation. On the other there is hypostatisation of the art work as the goal of the art process, and the relation between art work and individual as paramount. This necessarily leads to a dissolution of those social values which make the art in question a social relation, and therefore ultimately results in the art work's ceasing to be an art work and becoming a mere private phantasy.

All bourgeois art during the last two centuries shows the steady development of this bifurcation. As long as the social values inherent in an art form are not disintegrated – e.g. up to say 1910 – the artist who hypostatises the art form and despises the market can produce good art. After that, it becomes steadily more difficult. Needless to say, the complete acceptance of the market, being a refusal to regard any part of the art process as a social process, is even more incompetent to produce great art. Anything which helps the artist to escape from the bourgeois trap and become conscious of social relations inherent in art, will help to delay the rot. For this reason the novel is the last surviving literary art form in bourgeois culture, for in it, for reasons explained elsewhere, the social relations inherent in the art process are overt. Dorothy Richardson, James Joyce, and Proust, all in different ways are the last blossoms of the bourgeois novel, for with them the novel begins to disappear as an objective study of social relations and becomes a study of the subject's experience in society. It is then only a step for the thing experienced to disappear and, as in Gertrude Stein, for complete 'me-ness' to reign.

It is inevitable that at this stage the conception of the artist as a pure 'artist' must cease to exist. For commercialised art has become intolerably base and negated itself. And equally art for art's sake (that is, the ignoring of the market and concentration on the perfect art work as a goal in itself) has negated itself, for the art form has ceased to exist, and what was art has become private phantasy. It is for this reason that sincere artists, such as Lawrence, Gide, Romain Rolland, Romains and so on, cannot be content with the beautiful art work, but seem to desert the practice of art for social theory and become novelists of ideas, literary prophets and propaganda novelists. They represent the efforts of bourgeois art, exploded into individualistic phantasy and commercialised muck, to become once more a social process and so be reborn. Whether such art is or can be great art is beside the point, since it is inevitably the prerequisite for art becoming art again, just as it is beside the point whether the transition from bourgeoisdom to communism is itself smooth or happy or beautiful or free, since it is the inevitable step if bourgeois anarchy and misery is to be healed and society to become happy and free.

But what is art as a social process? What is art, not as a mere art work or a means of earning a living, but in itself, the part it plays in society? I have dealt fully with this point elsewhere, and need only briefly recapitulate now.

The personal phantasy or day-dream is not art, however beautiful. Nor is the beautiful sunset. Both are only the raw material of art. It is the property of art that it makes mimic pictures of reality which we accept as illusory. We do not suppose the events of a novel really happen, that a landscape shown on a painting can be walked upon – yet it has a measure of reality.

The mimic representation, by the technique appropriate to the art in question, causes the social representation to sweat out of its pores an affective emanation. The emanation is *in* us, *in* our affective reaction with the elements of the representation. Given in the representation are not only the affects, but, simultaneously, their organisation in an affective *attitude* towards the piece of reality symbolised in the mimicry. This affective attitude is bitten in by a general heightening of consciousness and increase in self-value, due to the non-motor nature of the innervations aroused, which seems therefore all to pass into an affective irradiation of consciousness. This affective attitude is not permanent, as is the intellectual attitude towards reality aroused by a cogent scientific argument, but still – because of the mnemic character-istics of an organism – it remains as an *experience* and must, therefore, in proportion to the amount of conscious poignancy accompanying the experience and the nature of the experience, modify the subject's general attitude towards life itself. This modification tends to make life more interesting to the organism, hence the survival value of art. But viewed from society's standpoint, art is the fashioning of the affective conscious-ness of its members, the conditioning of their instincts.

Language, simply because it is the most general instrument for communicating views of reality, whether affective and cognitive, has a particularly fluid range of representations of reality. Hence the suppleness and scope of literary art; the novel, the drama, the poem, the short story, and the essay. It can draw upon all the symbolic pictures of reality made by scientific, historical and discursive intellectual processes. Art can only achieve its purpose if the pictures themselves are made simultaneously to produce affect and organisation. Then, even as the artist holds up to us the piece of reality, it seems already glowing with affective colouring.

Reality constitutes for us our environment; and our environment, which is chiefly social, alters continuously – sometimes barely perceptibly, sometimes at dizzy speeds. The socially accepted pictures we make in words of reality cannot change as if they were reflections in a mirror. An object is reflected in a mirror. If the object moves the reflection moves. But in language reality is symbolised in unchanging words, which give a false stability and permanence to the object they represent. Thus they instantaneously photograph reality rather than reflect it. This frigid character of language is regrettable but it has its utilitarian purposes. It is probably the only way in which man, with his linear consciousness, can get a grip of fluid reality. Language, as it develops, shows more and more of this false permanence, till we arrive at the Platonic Ideas, Eternal and Perfect Words. Their eternity and perfection is simply the permanence of print and paper. If you coin a word or write a symbol to describe an entity or event, the word will remain 'eternally' unchanged even while the entity has changed and the event is no longer present. This permanence is part of the inescapable nature of symbolism, which is expressed in the rules of logic. It is one of the strange freaks of the human mind that it has supposed that reality must obey the rules of logic, whereas the correct view is that symbolism by its very nature has certain rules, expressed in the laws of logic, and these are nothing to do with the process of reality, but represent the nature of the symbolic process itself.

The artist experiences this discrepancy between language and reality as follows: he has had an intense experience of a rose and wishes to communicate his experience to his fellows in words. He wishes to say, 'I saw a rose'. But 'rose' has a definite social meaning, or group of meanings, and we are to suppose that he has had an experience with the rose which does not correspond to any of society's previous experiences of roses, embodied in the word and its history. His experience of the rose is therefore the negation of the word 'rose', it is 'not-rose' – all that in his experience which is not expressed in the current social meaning of the word 'rose'. He therefore says – 'I saw a rose like' – and there follows a metaphor, or there is an adjective – 'a heavenly rose' or a euphemism – 'I saw a flowery blush', and in each case there is a synthesis, for his new experience has become socially fused into society's old experiences and both have been changed in the process. His own experience has taken colour from all past meanings of the word 'rose', for these will be present in men's minds when they read his poem, and the word 'rose' will have taken colour from his individual experience, for his poem will in future be in men's minds when they encounter the word 'rose'.

But why was the poet's experience different from society's tradition? Because that cross-section of his environment which we call his individual life-experience was different. But if we take all society's art as a whole, i.e. the sum of individual cross-sections, we get on the one hand the whole experience of the environment averaged out, and also the average man, or average genotype. Now the constant genesis of new art must mean that the environment is changing, so that man's individual experiences are changing, and he is constantly finding inherited social conscious formulations inadequate and requiring re-synthesis. Thus if art forms remain unchanged and traditional, as in Chinese civilisation, it is evident that the environment – social relations – are static. If they decay, the environment is on the down-grade, as with current bourgeois culture. If they improve, the reverse is the case. But the artist's value is not in *self*-expression. If so, why should he struggle to achieve the synthesis in which old social formulations are fused with his individual experience? Why not disregard social formalities and express himself directly as one does by shouting, leaping, and cries? Because, to begin with, it is the old bourgeois illusion to suppose there is such a thing as pure individual expression. It is not even that the artist nobly forces his self-expression into a social mould for the benefit of society. Both attitudes are simply expressions of the old bourgeois fallacy that man is free in freely giving vent to his instincts. In fact the artist does not express himself in art forms, he finds himself therein. He does not adulterate his free self-expression to make it socially current, he finds free self-expression only in the social relations embodied in art. The value of art to the artist then is this, that it makes him free. It appears to him of value as a self-expression, but in fact it is not the expression of a self but the discovery of a self. It is the creation of a self. In synthesising his experience with society's, in pressing his inner self into the mould of social relations, he not only creates a new mould, a socially valuable product, but he also moulds and creates his own self. The mute inglorious Milton is a fallacy. Miltons are made, not born.

The value of art to society is that by it an emotional adaptation is possible. Man's instincts are pressed in art against the altered mould of reality, and by a specific organisation of the emotions thus generated, there is a new attitude, an *adaptation*.

All art is produced by this tension between changing social relations and outmoded consciousness. The very reason why new art is created, why the old art does not satisfy either artist or appreciator, is because it seems somehow out of gear with the present. Old art always has meaning for us, because the instincts, the source of the affects, do not change, because a new system of social relations does not exclude but includes the old, and because new art too includes the traditions of the art that has gone before. But it is not enough. We must have new art.

And new art results from tension. This tension takes two forms. (i) One is productive – the evolutionary form. The tension between productive relations and productive forces secures the advance of society as a whole, simply by producing in an even more pronounced form the contradiction which was the source of the dynamism. Thus bourgeois culture by continually dissolving the relations between men for relations to a thing, and thus hypostatising the market, procured the growth of industrial capitalism. And, in the sphere of art it produced the increasing individualism which, seen at its best in Shakespeare, was a positive value, but pushed to its limit finally spelt the complete breakdown of art in surréalism, Dadaism and Steinism.

(ii) The tension now becomes revolutionary. For productive relations are a brake on productive forces and the tension between them, instead of altering productive relations in the direction of giving better outlet to productive forces, has the opposite effect. It drives productive relations on still further into negation, increases the tension, and prepares the explosion which will shatter the old productive relations and enable them to be rebuilt anew – not arbitrarily, but according to a pattern which will itself be given by the circumstances of the tension. Thus in art the tension between individualism and the increasing complexity and catastrophes of the artist's environment, between the free following of dream and the rude blows of anarchic reality, wakes the artist from his dream and forces him in spite of himself to look at the world, not merely as an artist, but also as a man, as a citizen, as a sociologist. It forces him to be interested in things not strictly germane to art – politics, economics, science, and philosophy – just as it did during the early bourgeois Renaissance, producing 'all-round men' like Leonardo da Vinci. Whether this is good for art or not is beside the point. Bourgeois art like bourgeois culture is moribund and this process is an inevitable concomitant of the stage preceding art's rebirth. And because of this intervening period, the new art when it emerges will be art more conscious of itself as part of the whole social process, will be *communist* art. This explains why all modern artists of any significance such as Lawrence, Gide, Aragon, dos Passos, Eliot and so on, cannot be content to be pure artists, but must also be prophets, thinkers, philosophers, and politicians, men interested in life and social reality as a whole. They are conscious of having a message. This is the inevitable effect on art of a revolutionary period, and it is not possible to escape from it into 'pure' art, into the ivory tower, for now there is no pure art; that phase is either over or not yet begun.

But at a revolution two paths are possible. So indeed they are in evolution – one can either stay still and be classical, academic and null, or go forward. But at a time of revolution it is not possible to stay still, one must either go forward, or back. To us this choice appears as a choice between Communism and Fascism, either to create the future or to go back to old primitive values, to mythology, racialism, nationalism, hero-worship, and *participation mystique*. This Fascist art is like the regression of the neurotic to a previous level of adaptation.

It is Lawrence's importance as an artist that he was well aware of the fact that the pure artist cannot exist to-day, and that the artist must inevitably be a man hating cash relationships and the market, and profoundly interested in the relations between persons. Moreover, he must be a man not merely profoundly interested in the relations between persons as they are, but interested in changing them, dissatisfied with them as they are, and wanting newer and fuller values in personal relationships.

But it is Lawrence's final tragedy that his solution was ultimately Fascist and not Communist. It was regressive. Lawrence wanted us to return to the past, to the 'Mother'. He sees human discontent as the yearning of the solar plexus for the umbilical connexion, and he demands the substitution for sharp sexual love of the unconscious fleshy identification of foetus with mother. All this was symbolic of regression, of neurosis, of the return to the primitive.

Lawrence felt that the Europe of to-day was moribund; and he turned therefore to other forms of existence, in Mexico, Etruria and Sicily, where he found or thought he found systems of social relations in which life flowed more easily and more meaningfully. The life of Bourgeois Europe seemed to him permeated with possessiveness and rationalising, so that it had got out of gear with the simple needs of the body.

In a thousand forms he repeats this indictment of a civilisation which consciously – *and just because it is conscious* – sins against the instinctive currents which are man's primal source of energy. It is a mistake to suppose that Lawrence preaches the gospel of sex. Bourgeois Europe has had its bellyful of sex, and a sex cult would not now attract the interest and emotional support which Lawrence's teaching received. Lawrence's gospel was purely sociological. Even sex was too conscious for him:

Anybody who calls my novel (*Lady Chatterley's Lover*) a dirty sexual novel, is a liar. It's not even a sexual novel: it's a phallic. Sex is a thing that exists in the head, its reactions are cerebral, and its processes mental. Whereas the phallic reality is warm and spontaneous — '

Again he wrote:

What ails me is the absolute frustration of my primitive societal instinct ... I think societal instinct much deeper than the sex instinct – and societal repression much more devastating. There is no repression of the sexual individual comparable to the repression of the societal man in me, by the individual ego, my own and everybody else's. I am weary even of my own individuality, and simply nauseated by other people's.

One more analysis by him of the evil in bourgeois culture: (in the Cornish people) —

the old race is still revealed, a race which believed in the darkness, in magic, and in the magic transcendency of one man over another which is fascinating. Also there is left some of the old sensuousness of the darkness and warmth and passionateness of the blood, sudden, incalculable. Whereas they are like insects, gone cold, living only for money, for *dirt*. They are foul in this. They ought to die.

Now here is a clear artistic, i.e. *emotional*, analysis of the decay of bourgeois social relations. They live for money, the societal instinct is repressed, even the sex relations have become cold and infected. Survivals of barbaric social relations between men (the 'magic transcendency' of man over man) stand out as valuable in a culture where these relations have become relations between man and a thing, *man and dirt.*

But Lawrence does not look for a cause in social relations themselves, but in man's consciousness of them. The solution of the individual's needs is then plainly to be found in a return to instinctive living. But how are we to return to instinctive living? By casting off consciousness; we must return along the path we have come. But intellectualism consists in this, that we give either linguistically, plastically, or mentally, a symbolic projection to portions of reality, and consciousness or thinking consists simply in shuffling these images or verbal products. If therefore we are to cast off intellectualism and consciousness we must abandon all symbolism and rationalisation *tout court*, we must *be*, and no longer think, even in images. Yet on the contrary Lawrence again and again *consciously* formulates his creed in intellectual terms or terms of imagery. But this is self-contradiction, for how can we be led intellectually and consciously *back* from consciousness? It is our consciousness that Lawrence attempts to extend and heighten even at the moment he urges us to abandon it.

Consciousness can only be abandoned in action, and the first action of Fascism is the crushing of culture and the burning of the books. It is impossible therefore for an artist and thinker to be a consistent Fascist. He can only be like Lawrence, a self-contradictory one, who appeals to the consciousness of men to abandon consciousness.

There is a confusion here due to equating consciousness with thinking and unconsciousness with feeling. This is wrong. Both are conscious. No one ever had or could have an unconscious affect or emotion. Feeling indeed is what makes the unconscious memory-traces conscious, and heats them into thoughts. All of us, in times of deep feeling, whether artistic or emotional feeling, are aware of heightened consciousness almost like a white light in us so intense and clear is it. But Lawrence never clearly saw this, and constantly equates unconsciousness with feeling and consciousness with intellect. For example:

My great religion is a belief in the blood, in the flesh, as being wiser than the intellect. We can go wrong in our minds. But what our blood feels and believes and says is always true. The intellect is only a bit and a bridle. What do I care about knowledge? All I want is to answer to my blood, direct, without fumbling intervention of mind, or moral, or what not. I conceive a man's body as a kind of flame, like a candle flame forever upright and yet flowing: and the intellect is just the light that is shed on the things around, coming God knows how from out of practically nowhere, and being *itself,* whatever there is around it that it lights up. We have got so ridiculously mindful, that we never know that we ourselves are anything – we think there are only the objects we shine upon. And there the poor flame goes on burning ignored, to produce this light. And instead of chasing the mystery in the fugitive, half-lighted things outside us, we ought to look at ourselves and say, 'My God, I am myself!' That is why I like to live in Italy. The people are so unconscious. They only feel and want, they don't know. We know too much. No, we only *think* we know such a lot. A flame isn't a flame because it lights up two, or twenty objects on a table. It's a flame because it is itself. And we have forgotten ourselves.

Feeling and thinking play into each other's hands and heighten each other. Man feels more deeply than the slug because he thinks more. Why did Lawrence make this error of supposing them essentially exclusive, and equate feeling with unconsciousness? Once again, the answer is in the nature of current society. All feeling and all thinking must contain something of each other to form part of consciousness at all. But it is possible to distinguish certain conscious phenomena as chiefly feeling, or vice versa. 'Pure' feelings, any more than 'Pure' thoughts, do not exist at all, since the first would be a mere instinctive tendency, the second nothing but a mnemic trace. Both would be unconscious and evidenced therefore only in behaviour. Lawrence might mean that feeling has wilted under modern conditions and that we must expand the feeling basis of our consciousness.

We know this of feelings (and affects generally) that they come into consciousness associated with innate responses or – more loosely – that they seem to be born of the modification, by experience and in action of the 'instincts'. Instinct going out in unmodified action, in mechanical response to a stimulus, is without *feeling,* it is pure automatism. Only when it becomes modified by memory traces or stifled by action does it become conscious and appear as feeling. The more intelligent the animal, the more its behaviour is modifiable by experience, the more feeling it displays. This extra display of feeling is *because* it is more intelligent, more conscious, less swayed by heredity, more subject to personal experience. Modification of innate responses by experience simply implies that previous behaviour leaves a mnemic trace on the neurones, chiefly of the cortex. These when innervated produce a new pattern, whose modification takes in the cortical sphere the form of thoughts and, in the visceral and thalamic sphere, the form of feelings or emotional dynamism. The different proportion of the components decides whether we call them thoughts or feelings. Even the simplest thought is irradiated with affect, and even the simplest emotion is accompanied by a thought, not necessarily verbalised but of some such character as 'I am hurt', or 'A pain'. It is because thought and feeling arise from the same modification of innate responses, by experience, that the growth of intelligence, i.e. of the *capacity* for modification of behaviour by experience, is accompanied by a steadily increasing emotional complexity, richness, and deepness. It is plain that the growth of civilisation in *Homo Sapiens* has been accompanied by a steady increase in sensibility to pain and pleasure. This is the famous 'sensitiveness' of civilised man, the 'luxury' of high cultures, which is also manifested in their art and their vocabulary. Primitive peoples on the other hand show a marked deficiency in their sensibility, not only to refined emotions but even the cruder ones. The extremely erotic character of savage dances is not due, as some observers naïvely suppose, to the emotional erethism of the natives, but to the reverse, that in them the erotic impulses, owing to their deficient sensibility, can only be aroused by violent stimulation, whereas a slight stimulus will set off the hair-trigger emotions of civilised people. The same phenomenon is shown in primitive insensibility to pain. Consequently if we are to return down the path we have come from, back to primitiveness, to the blood, to the flesh, it is not only to less and cruder thought but also to less and cruder feeling, to a lessened consciousness in which feeling and thought, precisely because they are less rich and complex, will be more intimately mingled, until finally, as they both blend completely and become one, they vanish and nothing is left but unconscious *behaviour*. But how can this goal be of value to an artist, save on condition he denies himself the very law of his being? Art is not unconscious behaviour, it is conscious feeling.

It is, however, possible to broaden feeling without altering thought or losing consciousness, by altering the ratio between them in modern civilisation. That is precisely the purpose of art, for the artist makes use always of just those verbal or pictorial images of reality which are more charged with feeling than cognition, and he organises them in such a way that the affects reinforce each other and fuse to a glowing mass. Consequently, he who believes that at all costs the feeling element must be broadened in present-day consciousness, must preach and secure, not the contraction of all consciousness, but the widening of feeling consciousness. This is art's mission. Art is the technique of affective manipulation in relation to reality. Lawrence was doing what I suppose him to have wished to do, just when he was artist pure and simple, sensitively recording the spirit of a place or the emotions of real people – in his early work. In proportion as he became a prophet, preaching a gospel intellectually, he departed from that goal.

How did he come to make first the initial *sortie* in favour of feeling, and then the contradictory error, deserting art for preaching? He came to the first conclusion because feeling is impoverished by modern bourgeois culture. Social relations, by ceasing to be between man and man and adhering to a thing, become emptied of tenderness. Man feels himself deprived of love. His whole instinct revolts against this. He feels a vast maladaption to his environment. Lawrence perceives this clearly when he talks about the repression of the societal instinct.

But things have gone so far that no tinkering with social relations, no adaptation of the instincts to the environment by means of art, will cure this. Social relations themselves must be rebuilt. The artist is bound for the sake of his integrity to become thinker and revolutionary. Lawrence therefore was bound not to be content with pure art, with widening feeling consciousness in the old circle. He had to try and recast social relations and proceed to a solution. But there is only one revolutionary solution. Social relations must be altered, not so as to contract consciousness but so as to widen it. The higher feeling must be found, not in a lower but as always in a higher level of culture.

Naturally consciousness seems in bourgeois culture now, as in all periods of decay, full of defects with which being struggles, and this seems like unconsciousness crippled by consciousness. Those defects in bourgeois social relations all arise from the cash nexus which replaces all other social ties, so that society seems held together, not by mutual love or tenderness or obligation, but simply by profit. Money makes the bourgeois world go round and this means that selfishness is the hinge on which bourgeois society turns, for money is a dominating relation to an owned thing. This commercialisation of all social relations invades the most intimate of emotions, and the relations of the sexes are affected by the differing economic situations of man and woman. The notion of private property, aggravated by its importance and overwhelming power in bourgeois relations, extends to love itself. Because economic relations in capitalism are simply each man struggling for himself in the impersonal market, the world seems torn apart with the black forces of envy, covetousness and hate, which mix with and make ambivalent even the most 'altruistic' emotions.

But it is simplifying the drama to make it a struggle between contemporary consciousness and old being. It is a conflict between productive relations and productive powers, between the contemporary formulations of consciousness, and all the possibilities of future being including consciousness latent in society and struggling to be released from their bonds. Bourgeois defects are implicit in bourgeois civilisation and therefore in bourgeois consciousness. Hence man wants to turn against the intellect, for it seems that the intellect is his enemy, and indeed it is, if by intellect we mean the bourgeois intellect. But it can only be fought with intellect. To deny intellect is to assist the forces of conservatism. In hundreds of diverse forms we see to-day the useless European revolt against intellectualism.

In any civilisation the role of consciousness is to modify instinctive responses so that they flow smoothly into the mill of social relations and turn it. Instinct not money really turns the social mill, though in the bourgeois world instinctive relations can only operate along the money channel. Hence when social relations come to be a brake on society's forces, there is felt a conflict between the social relations and the instincts. It seems as if the feelings were out of gear, as if the world was uncomfortable and hurt the feelings and repressed them. It seems as if the instincts, and the feelings, those products of the instincts, were being penalised by the environment, and that, therefore, the instincts and feelings must be 'given their due', must be exalted even if it means breaking up and abandoning the civilised environment for a more primitive one. To-day this exaltation of the instincts is seen in all demands for a return to deeper 'feeling' as with Lawrence, and in all worships of unconscious 'mentation' as with the surréalists, Hemingways, and Fascists. In individuals this mechanism is infantile regression, seen in its pathological form in the neuroses.

Now these mechanisms involve the discovery of a real defect. Social being *is* held back by social consciousness; the instincts *are* thwarted and the feelings *are* made poor by the environment. But the remedy is wrong. The neurotic cannot, as we know, be cured by infantile regression. All it does for him is to secure him unconsciousness and take from him painful thoughts, at the price of a lowering of consciousness and an impoverish- ing of values. Civilisation cannot be cured by going back along the path to the primitive, it can only become at a lower level more unconscious of its decay. Just as the neurotic's return to childhood solutions of problems is unhealthier than childhood, so a civilisation's return to a primitive solution is unhealthier than primitive life itself. The very history between makes such solutions unreal. To the primitive these problems have never existed. To the regressive they have existed but he has repressed them. It is into the wilderness these people would lead us. They preach, not new vigour, but old decadence.

What then is the cure? We know that both in the case of the neurotic and the civilisation, the cure is a more strenuous and creative act than the invalid's relapse into the womb of that unconsciousness from which we emerged. Our task is to be performed, not in an air heavy and fetid with mysteries and dead symbolism like that of a cavern used for old obscene rites, but in the open air.

We are not to return to the old but it is into the new we must go; and the new does not exist, we must bring it into being. The child would love to return to the womb, but it must become adult and face the strenuous and bracing tasks of life. We are not to abandon consciousness but to expand it, to deepen and purge feeling and break up and recast thought, and this new consciousness does not exist in any thing's keeping either Mexicans or Yogis or the 'blood' but we must make it ourselves. In this struggle with reality in which instincts, feeling and thought all partake and interact, the instincts themselves will be changed, and emerging in consciousness as new thought and new feeling, will once again feel themselves in harmony with the new environment they have created. Social relations must be changed so that love returns to the earth and man is not only wiser but more full of emotion. This is not a task which one prophet can perform in one Gospel, but since the whole fabric of social relations are to be changed, every human being must in some sort participate in the change, be either for it or against it, and be victorious if he is for it and be defeated if he is against it.

Why did Lawrence, faced with the problem, fail of a solution? He failed because while hating bourgeois culture he never succeeded in escaping from its limitations. Here in him, too, we see the same old lie. Man is 'free' in so far as his 'free' instincts, the 'blood', the 'flesh' are given an outlet. Man is free not through but *in spite of* social relations.

If one believes this – which, as we have seen, is the deepest and most ineradicable bourgeois illusion, all others are built on this – one must, if one is hurt by bourgeois social relations, see security and freedom only in casting them off, and returning to a primitive state with less 'constraints'. One must necessarily believe freedom and happiness can be found by one's own individual action. One will not believe freedom and happiness can only be found through social relations, by co-operating with others to change them, but there is always something one can do, fly to Mexico, find the right woman or the right friends, and so discover salvation. One will never see the truth, that one can only find salvation for oneself by finding it for all others at the same time.

Lawrence therefore could never escape from this essential selfishness – not a petty selfishness but the selfishness which is the pattern of bourgeois culture and is revealed in pacifism, Protestantism, and all varieties of salvation obtained by individual action. The world to which Lawrence wished to return is not really the world of primitives who are in fact bound by more rigid relations than those of bourgeois Europe. It is the old bourgeois pastoral heaven of the 'natural man' born everywhere in chains, which does not exist. It does not exist because it is self-contradictory, and because it is self-contradictory the bourgeois world in striving for it more clearly produces the opposite, as in moving towards an object in a mirror we move away from the real object. Lawrence's gospel therefore only forms part of the self-destructive element in bourgeois culture.

Lawrence for all his gifts suffered from the old *petit bourgeois* errors. Like Wells, he strove to climb upwards into the world of bourgeois culture; being more artistic than Wells and born in a later era, it could not be the security and power of that already sick class that appealed to him. It was their cultural values. He succeeded in entering that world and drinking deeply of all its tremendous intellectual and aesthetic riches, only to find the riches turning into dust. The shock of that disillusion, added to the pain endured in that climb, filled him finally with a hatred for bourgeois values. He could criticise them relentlessly and bitterly, but he could provide no solution for the whole set of his life; all that long difficult climb of his into the bourgeois sunshine ensured that he remained a bourgeois. His was always bourgeois culture, conscious of its decay, criticising itself and with no solution except to go back to a time when things were different and so undo all the development that had brought bourgeois culture to this pass.

Had he been born later, had that sunlit world never appealed to him so irresistibly, he might have seen that it was the proletariat – to whom he was so near at the start of his climb – that was the dynamic force of the future. Not only would he then have had a standpoint outside bourgeois culture from which to criticise it, but from that position he would have been able to find the true solution – in the future, not the past. But Lawrence remained to the end a man incapable of that subordination of self to others, of co-operation, of solidarity as a class, which is the characteristic of the proletariat. He remained the individualist, the bourgeois revolutionary angrily working out his own salvation, critical of all, alone in possession of grace. He rid himself of every bourgeois illusion but the important one. He saw finally neither the world nor himself as it really was. He saw the march of events as a bourgeois tragedy, which is true but unimportant. The important thing, which was absolutely closed to him, was that it was also a proletarian renaissance.

Everywhere to-day will be found the conscious or unconscious followers of Lawrence – the pacifists, the snug little hedonists, the conscientious sexualists, the well-meaning Liberals, the idealists, all seeking the impossible solution, salvation through the free act of the individual will amid decay and disaster. They may find a temporary solution, a momentary happiness, although I judge Lawrence to have found neither. But it is of its nature unstable, for external events to which they have regressively adjusted themselves, beget incessantly new horrors and undreamed-of disasters. What avails such pinchbeck constructs during the screaming horror of a War? One may stop one's ears and hide oneself in Cornwall like Lawrence, but the cry of millions of suffering fellow-humans reaches one's ears and tortures one. And, the War at last survived, there come new horrors. The eating disintegration of the slump. Nazism outpouring a flood of barbarism and horror. And what next? Armaments piling up like an accumulating catastrophe, mass neurosis, nations like mad dogs. All this seems gratuitous, horrible, cosmic to such people, unaware of the causes. How can the bourgeois still pretend to be free, to find salvation individually? Only by sinking himself in still cruder illusions, by denying art, science, emotion, even ultimately life itself. Humanism, the creation of bourgeois culture, finally separates from it. Against the sky stands Capitalism without a rag to cover it, naked in its terror. And humanism, leaving it, or rather, forcibly thrust aside, must either pass into the ranks of the proletariat or, going quietly into a corner, cut its throat. Lawrence did not live to face this final issue, which would necessarily make straw of his philosophy and his teaching.

2

Freud:
A Study in Bourgeois Psychology

Freud is certain to be remembered and honoured as one of the pioneers of scientific psychology. But it is probable that like Kepler he will be regarded as a scientist who discovered important empirical facts but was unable to synthesise these discoveries except in a primitive semi-magical framework. Kepler with his divine Sun God, lived in the religious age of physics, Freud for all his honesty, lives in the mythical era of psychology: 'It may now be expected that the other of the "two heavenly forces", eternal Eros, will put forth his strength so as to maintain himself alongside of his equally immortal adversary.'

This is Freud's prognosis of the future of our civilisation. It is no bad symbolisation of the psychological trend of the present, but it will be seen that it is mythological symbolisation. Examination of the remainder of his psychology shows that it is generally religious in its presentation. It is a psychology of forces and personifications. Freud is no exceptional psychologist here. Psychology still awaits its Newton. At least Freud has refused to accept the outworn shams of Christianity or of idealistic metaphysics. In *The Future of an Illusion* he maintains the fruitful materialistic traditions of bourgeois science, which bourgeois science itself to-day as it loses its grip is deserting. The metaphysical psychology with its memory, reason, conation, perception, thought, and feeling which Freud helped to destroy is more mythological than Freudism. This psychology, of which Freudism is an enemy, belongs to an even earlier age of science. It reduces mentation to verbiage, and then the organisation of this verbiage is called thought. It is, however, real mentation with which Freud deals always, only he symbolises the inner structure of this neurological behaviour in terms of real entities as glamorous and personal as the Olympian gods of old. The Censor, the Ego, the Super-ego, the Id, the Oedipus complex, and the Inhibition are mind-deities, like the weather deities who inhabited Greek Olympus. Freud's picture of a struggle between eternal Eros and eternal Thanatos, between the life and death instincts, between the reality principle and the pleasure principle, is only the eternal dualism of reflective barbarians, carried over by Christianity from Zoroastrianism, and now introjected by Freud into the human mind. It represents a real struggle but in terms of a Western bourgeois myth.

As confirmation of his fable about Zeus, the Greek could point to the thunder and lightning. As confirmation of the endless war between Ormuzd and Ahriman, the Parsee could remind the sceptic of the endless warfare that tears life in twain. Freudians point to the psychic phenomena of dreams, hysteric and neurotic symptoms, obsessions and slips of the pen and tongue as confirmation of their intricate mythology. The early scientists could claim the fall of every stone as the evidence of the mysterious force of gravity and all phenomena of heat and cold as testimony to the passage of a mysterious 'caloric'. In Freudism 'libido' plays the part of the mythical 'caloric' of eighteenth-century heat mechanics, or of the 'gravity' of Newtonian physics.

It may be argued with some reason that psychology is an appropriate sphere for fables and emotive symbolisation, but this claim withdraws it from the circle of science to that of art. It is better to demand that mythical psychology should exist only in the novel and that psychology should be a science. If so, the obligation falls upon psychoanalysts either to leave any empirical facts they have discovered in thin air for some abler mind to fit into a causal scheme, as Newton co-related Kepler's separate and arbitrary laws of planetary motion, or else they must clearly exhibit the causality of their discoveries without recourse to mythological entities. This Freud and his followers have failed to do. Thus instead of being causal and materialistic, their psychology is religious and idealistic. Yet Freud is a materialist and is clearly aware of the illusory content of religion. But he is also a bourgeois. This class outlook affects his psychology through certain implicit assumptions from which he starts, assumptions that appear in all bourgeois culture as a disturbing yet invisible force, just as Uranus until discovered was for us only a mysterious perturbation in the orbits of the known planets. These implicit assumptions are firstly that the consciousness of men is *sui generis*, unfolding like a flower from the seed instead of being a primarily social creation, and secondly that there is a source of free action in the individual, the 'free will' the 'wish', or the 'instincts', which is only free in proportion to the extent to which it is unrestrained by social influences. These two assumptions are of vital significance for psychology, and just because they are implicit, they act like buried magnets, distorting all Freud's psychology and making it an unreal kind of a science tainted with wish-fulfilment.

Freud has been exceptionally unfortunate in that his school of psychology has been rent repeatedly by schisms. Jung and Adler are the most notable schismatics, but almost every psychoanalyst is a heretic in embryo. Now this must necessarily have been a matter for sorrow to Freud, although he has borne it as calmly as he has borne the numerous attacks from all with vested interests in contemporary morality whom his discoveries seemed to menace. The Freudian schisms are not paralleled in other sciences. The disciples of a discoverer of new empirical principles, such as the disciples of Darwin, Newton and Einstein, do not as a rule turn and rend him. They work within the general limits of his formulations, merely enrichening and modifying them, without feeling called upon to attack the very foundations on which the structure is based.

Freud is himself indirectly to blame. Schism is the hall-mark of religion, and a man who treats scientific facts as does Freud, in a religious way, must necessarily expect the trials and tribulations, as well as the intense personal relationships, of a religious leader. In approaching science in a religious spirit, I do not mean in a 'reverent' spirit. The scientist necessarily approaches reality, with all its richness and complexity, with a feeling of reverence and insignificance which is the more intense the more 'materialistic' he is, and, the less he feels that this reality is a mere offshoot or emanation of a Divine friend of his. I mean by a 'religious' approach, the belief that scientific phenomena are adequately explained by any symbolisation which includes and accounts for the phenomena. Thus 'caloric' accounts for temperature phenomena. None the less, no such mysterious stuff exists. In the same way Freud supposes that any fable which includes a connected statement of genuine psychical phenomena is a scientific hypothesis, whether or not it exhibits in a causal manner the inner relations of the phenomena. Of course such explanations break down because they do not fit into the causal scheme of science as a whole.

Now this is precisely the way religion sets about explaining the world: thunder and lightning are caused by deities. The world exists because it was created by a God. Disaster is the will of an omnipotent deity, or the triumph of an evil deity over an omnipotent deity. We die because we sinned long ago. Moreover, religion naïvely supposes that the fact that there is thunder and lightning, that the world exists, that disaster occurs in it, and that we die, is a proof that deities exist, that God created the world, and that we sinned long ago. This is what theologians mean by the Cosmological and Teleological proofs of God's existence. But this kind of 'proof' was long ago banished from science, and it is strange to see a man of Freud's intellectual gifts impressed by it. It is a sign of the crisis reached in bourgeois culture when psychology cannot escape from this kind of thing.

It follows from presuming that an adequate explanation of certain facts will be furnished by any fable connecting these facts, that for any group of facts an indefinite number of myths can be advanced as an explanation. Thus an indefinite number of religions exist which explain with different myths the same facts of man's unhappiness, his cruelty, his aspirations, his sufferings, his inequality and his death. Religion by its method of approach spawns schisms. The only reason that Churches can exist without disintegration is because of their material foundations in the social relations of their time.

Science can recognise only explanations which with as little symbolisation as possible exhibit the mutual determination of the phenomena concerned, and their relation with the rest of reality. Thus one scientific hypothesis is intolerant. It drives out another.

Scientific explanations, because of their austere structure, are not equally good, as different religions are equally good. One or other must go to the wall. And the test is simple. If, of two hypotheses one exhibits more comprehensively and less symbolically the structure of the determinism of the phenomena it explains and their relation to the already established structure of reality, that hypothesis will be more powerful as an instrument for predicting the recurrence of such phenomena in real life. Hence arises the crucial test, which decides between one hypothesis and another. For example, the crucial tests of the Einstein theory, as compared with the Newtonian, were the bending of light, the perturbation of planetary orbits, the increase of mass of alpha particles, and the shifts of the spectra of receding stars. But it is never possible to demonstrate by a crucial test the rival truths of the Protestant and Catholic theories, simply because they deal with entities assumed to be outside the structure of determined reality. The crucial test of the two theories is presumed to occur at the Last Judgement, that is, never in this life. The theories are expressly so formulated that it is not, for example, possible to test the Eucharist by chemical analysis. The Catholic theory states that in being turned into Christ's body the bread retains all the chemical and physical properties of ordinary bread. In the same way the Protestant theory makes it pointless to test for the salvation of a soul, precisely because the soul is asserted to be completely non-material and therefore inaccessible to determinism.

No hypothesis, religious or scientific, can have any meaning unless it can give rise to a crucial test, which will enable it to be socially compared with other hypotheses. Thought must interact with external reality to be of value or significance. Capitalist and socialist economists dispute as meaninglessly as theologians, as long as they base their defences of the rival systems on justice, liberty, man's natural equality, or any other 'rights'. No one has yet devised an instrument to measure or determine justice, equality, or liberty. The Marxian can be concerned only with the structure of concrete society and he will on this basis advance socialism as a superior form of organisation at a certain period of history because it permits a more efficient use of the means of material production. This makes possible the crucial test of practice – is communism more productive than capitalism? Thus economics remains scientific because it remains in the sphere of reality and does not deal with entities that cannot be determined quantitatively. For this reason, historical materialism has not given rise to as many brands of socialism as there are theorists. It can only be opposed by an hypothesis more penetrative of reality. The 'cast-iron inflexible dogmatism' of the communist corresponds to the scientists' 'rigid' and universal adherence to a methodological principle, such as the conservation of energy, until a fresh hypothesis, capable of a crucial test, has shown the need for its expansion or modification.

When we see a scientific 'school' rent by schism, or engaged in vigorous persecution, we may assume that a certain amount of the religious spirit has entered its science. Science has never been wholly free of it, but it has rent psychoanalysis into fragments.

Adler, Freud and Jung deal with the same mental phenomena. They are as follows: psychic phenomena consist of innervations of some of which we, as subjects, have a privileged (subjective) view. Some of these innervations, the smallest and most recent group phylogenetically, form a group often called the consciousness, the ego, or the subject. This group appears to be more self-determined than the other groups but all affect each other and form a kind of hierarchic process. Those which do not form part of the consciousness are called unconscious. At the moment of birth, the neurones capable of innervation exhibit certain specific patterns of innervation, involving certain specific somatic behaviour, as a result of internal and external stimuli. These patterns are known as 'the instincts'. But the experience resulting from the awakening of these patterns modifies, by means of a phenomenon which may be called 'memory' but is not peculiar to consciousness, the patterns themselves. At any moment of time, therefore, the system as a whole has a slightly different resonance or totality of patterns as a result of previous behaviour due to the then totality of patterns. The result will be to increase with lapse of time the range and complexity of the behaviour response to reality, and the hierarchy of groups of possible innervation combinations. We say, therefore, in ordinary language, that in the course of life a man learns by experience, or, a little more technically, that his instincts are modified or conditioned by situations. Such expressions contain a certain amount of mythology, perhaps at present unavoidable. In particular, the more autonomous group called the 'consciousness', in whose language all explanations of other less autonomous groups must be phrased, will necessarily tend to write everything from its angle, and give a peculiar twist to the description. Science itself is a product of consciousness.

Experiment leads us to believe that the innervations concerned in consciousness are phylogenetically the most recent in evolution, and that the older the neurone groups, the less modifiable they are in their behaviour, i.e. the less they are able to 'learn' by 'experience'. Hence they may be described as more infantile, primitive, bestial, archaic, or automatic, according to the mythological language one is adopting at the time.

In every innervation, however simple, the whole system of neurones is really concerned. If we play a chord on the piano, the strings we do not strike are as much concerned as those we do, because the chord is what it is being part of the well-tempered scale, and to the chord contribute also the wood, the air of the room, and our ears. Though consciousness deals with psychic phenomena in its own terms, yet in all conscious phenomena the innervations of the rest of the system are concerned and their innate responses, modified or unmodified, give all behaviour, including conscious phenomena, the 'ground' of their specific pattern. Hence we may say that the Unconscious modifies all behaviour, including consciousness; that is, that unconscious innervation and experience are a part of consciousness.

The study of this modification of the consciousness by the Unconscious is naturally of great interest to our consciousness. To understand it we must know accurately the innate responses of all parts of the nervous system, and the laws of their harmony. Sometimes as a result of the temporary instability of the conscious innervation pattern (e.g. in situations of emergency or difficulty or in sleep), the tune of behaviour is called chiefly by the phylogenetically older neurones, and these, as we saw, were less teachable than the newer groups. We then have behaviour in which there is a return to the earlier and less experienced state, the so-called infantile regression. In it some of life's experience is thrown away. We may also call this behaviour instinctive.

Now these disturbances have been studied by Freud, and he has made some interesting empirical discoveries about them. He has shown how much more common they are than we suspect and has elaborated a technique for detecting them. All his discoveries have been embodied in an elaborate and ingenious myth, or series of myths. This is due partly to the fact that he has not taken his own doctrine seriously. He has not realised that, since it is consciousness which is formulating psychoanalysis, all unconscious phenomena are likely to appear as seen by consciousness, not as causal phenomena with the same physiological basis as consciousness and ultimately homogeneous with it, but as wicked demons which burst into the neat, ordered world of consciousness. Just as causal phenomena, such as thunder and lightning, which burst into the accustomed world of the primitive, were attributed to the arbitrary acts of deities, so unconscious 'influences', causing perturbations in the conscious world, are by Freud called by such rude names as distortion, inhibition, regression, obsession, the id, the censor, the pleasure-principle, Eros, libido, the death instinct, the reality principle, a complex, a compulsion. Freud does not perceive the implications of the physiological content of his theory. All innervation patterns consist of an innate response (instinct) modified by experience (inhibition), and thus all innervation patterns contain varying proportions of conscious and unconscious elements, connected in various ways, but all forming the one circuit, overtly visible in behaviour. Freud has accepted for this part of his theory the prejudiced view of consciousness. He treats all unconscious components of behaviour as perturbations, distortions, or interferences, just as the treble part in music might regard the bass as distortion by some primitive unconsciousness. Just as mythological and consistent a psychology as Freud's might be written from the point of view of the 'unconscious' in which, instead of the 'instincts', the 'experiences' would now play the part of energetic imprisoned demons distorting or inhibiting the stability and simple life of the innate responses. And, in fact, when Freud comes to treat civilisation and man as a whole, he does swing over to this point of view. It is now experience or consciousness (culture) which is thwarting or distorting instinct (the unconscious). Naturally, therefore, Freud's doctrine contains a dualism which *cannot* be resolved.

But of course both consciousness and unconsciousness, as sharply distinct entities, are abstractions. In all the innervations which are part of behaviour, a varying proportion make up the group which at any time we call the consciousness or the ego. And they are not separate; consciousness is made vivid and given its content by the unconscious innervations, whose contribution we know consciously only as affect. A thought without affect is unconscious; it is simply one of the cortical neurones mnemically modified, but not at that moment affectively glowing, and therefore not part of the live circuit of unconsciousness. It is only an unconscious memory. Equally, an unconscious innervation or affect without memory is not an affect at all, but simply an instinctive reflex, a tendency unmodified by experience. Consciousness and unconsciousness are not exclusive opposites, but in any hierarchy of innervations forming the behaviour of the moment we have a certain amount with high mnemic modifiability and others with high innate predisposition, and the proportion of these may be varying. But they are in mutual relation, like the positive and negative poles of a battery activating a circuit, and it is only by abstraction that we separate out the complex called consciousness, as we might separate out the threads forming the pattern on a tapestry. The same threads pass through to the other side and form the reverse pattern there, the unconscious, and each pattern determines the other.

Freud gave to these discoveries of his, which were founded on the previous work of Charcot, Janet, Morton Prince, and Bleuler, formulations drawn from his consciousness, without the rigorous causality demanded in physical or chemical hypotheses. As a result, Freud's terminology consists of little but the abusive names coined by the consciousness for its distortion by the unconscious, or of the pitiful complaints by the unconscious of its modification by the experience embodied in conscious innervations. On the whole, our sympathies will be with the consciousness, for the consciousness represents recent experience, and recent experience is the richest; but reality reminds us that we cannot simply live in the new experience of the present. If we do, we shall be unable to advance beyond it; we shall be trapped in the limitations of the present. We must accept the present more thoroughly than that, we must accept the past *included* in the present. That does not mean that we must accept the past as the past, for, in being included in the present, it is changed. That indeed is what each present is in relation to the precedent past, it is that precedent past modified by the impression of an additional experience; and that present itself becomes the past when it is synthesised in a new present. This may sound metaphysical, and yet in the human body we see it given a 'crude' and material physiological basis. Everything below the optic thalamus represents the inherited experience of the ancestral past. The cerebrum is the organ for storing each present as it becomes the past, and sensory perception is the process by which the past, acquiring new experience, becomes the present. This ingression gives rise to the will, to the future.

Thus though we accept consciousness as latest and richest, we must not reject the Unconscious, as the worship of consciousness may too easily lead us to do. Those who accept consciousness only are entrapped in immediate experience, and can never progress to a richer consciousness; just as those who ignore the past in the present in the form of history are unable to grasp the richer future, which they write only in terms of the barren present. This is the lesson of historical materialism, that the future is not contained in the present, but in the present *plus* the past.

Still less can we accept *only* the past. That is worse than the other, it is a return to outworn things, it is infantile regression. It is the path that perpetually appeals to man when, as to-day, his consciousness seems to fail him at the tasks with which he is faced, but it is the way of defeat. The Unconscious has its wisdom, certainly, for it contains the condensed experience of ages of evolution, stamped in by natural selection. Our life is built on the foundations of the somatic wisdom of unconscious innervations. None the less, the spear-point of life's insertion into reality is the present, it is new experience and this new experience is unseizable by unconsciousness. It *is* consciousness.

Freudism does not accept the story of one party to the exclusion of the other's. It accepts *both* uncritically, and so involves itself in an irreconcilable dualism. After showing how the wicked complex-devils of the Unconscious distort and obsess consciousness, Freud goes over to the other side and paints the Unconscious as it would like to paint itself. He shows us the Instincts tortured by the inhibitions of culture, martyrs to the present and to consciousness. Yet the scientist ought in these matters to be impartial, otherwise he will never synthesise these two opposites, past and present, new and old. Freud raises only the barren trichotomy of metaphysics: (i) infantile regression (or worship of the past); (ii) conservatism (or blind acceptance of the present); (iii) dualism (the conception of present and past as eternal antagonists). Only the man who sees how the past is included in the present, can proceed to the future, child of a 'Marriage of Heaven and Hell'. They are included in the primary process of becoming, exhibited in the organism as active behaviour, in which unconscious and conscious innervations are the bass and treble of the innervation harmony in whose theme we distinguish instinct, thought, feeling and conation.

Directly Freud clothed the elements of this harmony in the fabulous and emotional symbols of psychoanalysis, Freud invited schism. Jung and Adler have invented symbols which are at least as good explanations of the same phenomena, and yet they are totally opposed to each other and to Freud's in their significance. In Adler's fable, the sexual 'instinct' makes hardly any appearance, yet his 'instinct of self-preservation' explains everything as satisfactorily as Freud's 'libido'. Since separate entities – such as an instinct of self-preservation or a Censor – are fabulous descriptions of certain innate physiological responses, it is not possible to find a crucial experiment to judge between Adler and Freud. They are disputing about myths, though the myths refer to real phenomena. In the same way Grecians might have disputed about inconsistencies in rival accounts of the birth of Athene from Zeus's head. What was actually being discussed by them was the modification of behaviour by experience or – more picturesquely – the Birth of Wisdom. Since both Athene and Zeus were mere symbolic fictions, such disputes about them were wasted time. Adler, Jung and Freud have wasted much of their time in precisely the same way.

Of them all Jung is perhaps the most scientific theoretically, even if he has made fewer empirical discoveries, because he does realise the dualism inherent in Freud's approach. But he never escapes from that dualism. On the contrary, he makes it the foundation of his theories.

————

So far we have been concerned with psychology as shown by the organism's behaviour, and have neglected the environment except as simple stimulus. Restricting our study to the organism, we regard all psychic phenomena as simply certain patterns of innervations. Some of these innervations in ourselves are consciousness. As a whole, they are part of a body's behaviour and we see part of this behaviour overtly as action, in ourselves or others. In the act of behaviour, the basic innervation patterns become modified. Thus the tune of a man's life begins with a simple hereditary phrase, on which experience plays endless variations, continually increasing, in richness and subtlety. This is part of the fact that a man's life is lived in Reality, whose nature it is that each new present includes the previous past, so growing increasingly in complexity.

But all behaviour is interaction between body and stimuli from outside, or between one part of the body and another. The organism never behaves alone; there is always an 'other', the environment, which is a party to its behaviour. Moreover the environment too has its history, for it is subject to time. Thus it is never the same environment; and each transaction the organism has with it is subtly different because since the previous transaction it has become more full of history. Hence the behaviour of the organism is a counter-point, in which the organism furnishes one part and the environment the other part. We may for purposes of analysis consider the melody of each separately, but actually behaviour is not a melody but a harmony. Thus the harmony of the psyche is itself a reflection of the harmony of the body's being in reality. The treble of the consciousness is a reflection of the melody of the environment; the bass of the unconsciousness is a reflection of the melody of the organism. The fundamental principle of physics is that each action has an equal and opposite reaction. Thus, after each act of behaviour, in which organism and environment interact, environment has affected organism and organism environment, and the resulting positions of each are different. Indeed that is why there is history, for the environment itself is simply a collection of mutually-interacting bodies. In between the act of an organism one moment and its act the next, the environment has changed, simply because the elements of which the environment is composed have interacted and changed each other.

Now of all known organisms, the human organism is the most elaborate in its melody and the most sensitive in its reaction to intercourse with reality. It is the organism which learns most from behaviour, from experience. Nothing changes so quickly as the human organism. In the same way the social environment, because the organisms of which it consists are chiefly human beings, also changes most quickly in between the acts of a human being. The study of this dialectic change is psychology from the point of view of the individual; but from the point of view of the sum of human beings, it is sociology or history, and in its causal statement it must include all portions of the environment with which human beings interact, even the fixed stars. But since in the short periods usually studied, cosmical conditions do not change importantly, they may be neglected. They might become important in a study of humanity which included the Ice Ages. Of primary interest to history are however the material elements in the environment that do change rapidly in the periods generally studied, i.e. machines, transport, cities, and, in brief, all the social relations arising from social production, for the change in the organism will necessarily be related to these changing features in its environment. The organism does not enter consciously or of its own will into these relations. They are prior and determine its consciousness and will. It is in fact impossible to study psychology without a background of sociology. If one does do so, either it is impossible to find the causal connexion in the change of the human psyche, or else one accepts the human psyche as unchanging and all laws discovered from a study of contemporary psyches seem true for all time.

As it happens, no modern school of psychology has ever studied social relations as primary, as conditioning the consciousness which is generated by them. None study concrete society and its non-psychical basis. No modern school of psychology has ever yet got so far as to formulate its basic approach to the environment of the psyche it studies, continuous interaction with which is the law of psychic life.

Freud approaches his psychological problems with the assumptions of a bourgeois idealist, to whom nothing exists of reality save an unchanging backcloth before which the ideas play their parts. It is true that these ideas are now rather like the 'ruling passions' of older philosophers, and have been given the name of 'the instincts' or 'Libido', but the story is still the same fabulous drama, in which are performed the 'miracles' of inhibitions, sublimation, cathexis, narcissism, transformation and displacement, by those good and bad fairies, the censor, the ego, the super-ego and the id. There are even cannibal instincts and incest instincts, though it staggers the imagination of the biologist to infer how these variations evolved and became hereditary. There is no causality.

Freud imagines a pleasure-principle attempting to gain freedom for its pleasures within the bounds of the prison house of reality. Beyond those bounds of causality we must not stray, Freud admits, but inside their ever-contracting boundaries there appears to be true freedom. It is a fine fable. The instincts, like bourgeois revolutionaries, desperately attempt to gratify themselves, oppressed by the tyrant Reality's laws. Has such a conception any place in science?

Freud, like all bourgeois intellectuals, like Eddington, Russell and Wells, cannot lose his faith that there is a separate cell called liberty, mysteriously existing in the granite of scientific causality. Scientific thought is continually (it is supposed) contracting the dimensions of this chamber of little ease, but still it exists.

In particular, these thinkers suppose that man is more free, more at liberty, the more he is free from the pressure of culture, consciousness and social organisation. Russell, Eddington, Freud and Wells are alike in this supposition, which, carried (as they do not carry it) to the logical conclusion, means that the only beings with real liberty are the unconscious brutes.

But the truth is, the world is not a prison house of reality in which man has been allotted by some miracle a honey cell of pleasure. Man is a part of reality, in constant relation with it, and the progress of consciousness, in so far as it increases his knowledge of causality, increases his freedom. In the same way, civilisation increases his freedom, in so far as it increases his causal control over reality, including himself. In this last, in the self-control of men as compared with their environmental control by machines, we are least advanced, and this is precisely because psychology, which would show us how to control ourselves, is always trying to evade causality. Science does not seem to be telling man about freedom. On the contrary, it seems only to be discovering cast-iron laws, of whose existence and rigidity he did not guess. But is an animal in a cage free because it does not realise it is a cage? Will it not only become free when it realises that a locked cage completely restricts its movements and that to be free it must *necessarily* unlock the door?

Bourgeois civilisation is built on this rock, that complete freedom consists in complete personal anarchy, and that man is *naturally* completely free. This Rousseauism is found distorting all bourgeois thought. Freud cannot help visualising civilisation as the enslavement of the completely free instincts by culture.

Hence the honest bourgeois is always either pessimistic or religious. Man must have some conscious social organisation to exist socially (police, judges, factories, education), and all these seem to him so many limits to his freedom, not because of the *imperfection* of the organisation, which is the communist criticism, but because there is organisation at all. Thus to the bourgeois, civilisation seems damned by its premises and there is no hope in this life of attaining freedom. All organisation, all consciousness, all thought eventually seem to the bourgeois intellectual the corruption or inhibition or repression of the completely free natural man; but this natural man is an anthropoid ape, for man without society is a brute.

Can we talk of the inhibition or repression of that which is not free? And are the instincts free or are they, as we see so clearly in the insect, blind mechanical enslavements, deaf to individual learning, heeding only the slow ancestral experience of the species? Then society, creating by its 'inhibitions' and 'repressions' *consciousness*, is leading the instincts on the path not of slavery but of freedom. To call, as Freud does, that which frees the enslaved instincts 'inhibitions' or 'repression' is prejudiced.

Freud sees in the evolution of each individual psyche nothing but the drama of the instincts fighting among themselves, and so giving rise to the repressions of culture. He sees in culture nothing but the projection of this drama into the environment, on a collective scale: 'And now,' he says, 'it seems to me, the meaning of the evolution of culture is no longer a riddle to us. It must present to us the struggle between Eros and Death, between the instincts of life and the instincts of destruction, as it works itself out in the human species.' Thus to him culture is autonomously psychic, and without internal causality, just because it has no external connexion. The material environment is ignored.

In another passage he attributes the organisations of society to the identifications of all individuals with each other through the father, thus explaining both social cohesion and leadership. And he adds (explaining our present discontents): 'This danger (i.e. social discontent) is most menacing where the social forces of cohesion consist predominantly of identifications of the individuals of the group with one another, whilst leading personalities fail to acquire the significance that should fall to them in the process of group-formation.' Here bourgeois idealism, long before the advent of Hitler, unwittingly writes the charter of barbarous Fascism, Fuhrership, and the Corporate State. Withdrawing from the future, Fascism appeals to a savage past for salvation. By a strange irony, Freud becomes the apologist of the Fascist philosophy which rejects him, which burns his books, and seems repugnant to him. Yet this is the irony of all bourgeois culture, that because it is based on a contradiction, it gives rise to the opposite of what it desires. It desires freedom and individual expression, but, because it believes freedom is to be found in abolition of social organisation, it gives rise to all the tyrannies and blind crippling necessities of the modern world. Freudism, attempting to cure civilisation of its instinctive distortions, points the way to Nazism.

Is Freud, then, an ally of Fascism, whose psychological mechanism in the individual his theory explains and condemns? In one sense, yes! As bourgeois consciousness breaks down before new reality, it is aware of its failure and this sense of failure is itself a disintegrating force. It is part of the role of Freud to make overt the rottenness in bourgeois social relations, but there are no 'absolutely hopeless' situations, and bourgeois culture defends itself from these humiliating awarenesses by the mechanism of barbaric pseudo-religious constructs, such as that of Fascist ideology. When consciousness reveals its inadequacy to a situation, one can either advance to a wider consciousness which will include the new situation that brought about the crisis, or one can regress to a former solution of a similar problem in the childhood of the individual or the nation. This is the mechanism of neuroses. But this is no solution, for the old situation is not the same situation, and the mind that faces it too has changed. So one gets only a false and pathological infantilism, full of illusion and phantasy. Freudism can point this out but, because of its lack of a scientific basis, it cannot show the way to attain the wider consciousness. Thus, after all, it is not a therapy, it is only a diagnosis. The analyst vainly exposes the regressive nature of the neurotic's solution, if he cannot himself provide a better solution. And Freud cannot. We can only cast out error with truth, and Freud had no new truth to offer, only a fairy-tale recording the breakdown of bourgeois civilisation as seen in its own mythological terms.

In answer to criticism of Freud's mythology, it has often been urged that Freudism is a therapy, not a science. Such defenders admit that emotively-charged concepts such as libido, the censor, the Oedipus complex and inhibition have no place in a scientific hypothesis. But (they argue) the neurosis is an emotional crisis, and the neurotic can only be cured emotionally. It is no use talking to him about conditioned reflexes. His emotions must be stirred, and this justifies the myths of psychoanalysis, by which truths are conveyed to him fabulously but vividly.

But just because Freudism is not a science, it fails as a therapy. Granted that the neurotic must be touched emotionally, are individual psychoanalysts really arrogant enough to believe that the enormous, creative force of emotion, the dynamism of society, can be directed by them, as individuals, and by means of such arid concepts as those of Freudism? Emotion, in all its vivid colouring, is the creation of ages of culture acting on the blind unfeeling instincts. All art, all education, all day-to-day social experience, draw it out of the heart of the human genotype and direct and shape its myriad phenomena. Only society as a whole can really direct this force in the individual. To imagine that one psychoanalyst can shape it is to believe that one can bring down the houses of London with a shout. Could any discipline rooted in scientific causality have made so rash a misjudgement of the powers of the individual, as to believe that the mighty social force of emotion could be harnessed by 'transference of libido' to the earnest, middle-aged and bald physician? At least the Victorian heroine who wished to reform the sinner by a good woman's love had personal charm and unlimited opportunity.

The innate responses of an organism, the so-called instincts, as such are unconscious, mechanical, and unaffected by experience. Psychology therefore is not concerned with them, for they are the material of physiology. Psychology, in its study of consciousness or unconsciousness, can only have for its material all those psychic contents that results from the *modification* of responses by experience. It is this material that changes, that develops, that is distinctively human, that is of importance, and psychology should and in practice does ignore the *unchanging* instinctual basis as a cause. It concerns itself with the variable, which changes not only from age to age but from individual to individual and in an individual from hour to hour.

Reflexes are conditioned by experience, by action upon the environment. In man the environment consists of society, and action of education, daily work, daily life, what man sees, eats, hears, handles, travels in, co-operates in, loves, reverences, is repelled by – the whole fabric of social relations. These, in the developing instinctual organism, produce the psyche, give consciousness its contents and the unconscious its trend, and make man what he is. Consciousness is the organ of social adaptation, but society is not composed of consciousnesses.

It is true that each contact of organism with the environment not only affects the organism but also affects the environment. But in studying any one psyche, which is the task of individual psychology, we see on the one hand a naked genotype, dumb, ignorant and without tradition, whereas, on the other hand, forming its environment, we see not only millions of other individuals but the formulation in bricks and mortar, in social organisations, in religions, sciences, laws and language of the experience of aeons of human activity. Consequently the action of the organism upon this mass of consciousness is minute compared with its reaction upon the organism, except in those cases where, owing to its own instability, the smallest touch is already sufficient to send it over violently into a new position. Such touches are administered by Marx. But in formulating a scientific psychology as in formulating a mechanics, the spectacular side is of no importance compared to the underlying causal laws, good for the ordinary as well as the exceptional event. The fact that in certain conditions of instability a cricket ball could cause the sun to explode, does not justify us in imagining that cricket balls exert forces greater than suns. In psychology, as in mechanics, the reaction of a body on its cosmic environment can be neglected, as compared to the effect of the world on the body.

Thus psychology must be extracted from sociology, not *vice versa*. For sociology, if scientific (and the only school of scientific sociology was founded by Marx), already includes the conscious formulations and the material accretions, arising from the dialectic of social relations, which provide the environment of the developing infant psyche. These are the social relations into which the organism enters irrespective of its will. The single organism is a slave to its environment, just as the particle is a slave to time and space, in spite of the fact that the social environment is composed of the activities of human organisms and time and space are the sum of the relations of particles. We must establish sociology before we can establish psychology, just as we must establish the laws of time and space before we can treat satisfactorily of a single particle. This is not to say that psychology and sociology are the same. Psychology has a province of tremendous importance to the human race, but it can only be studied scientifically on a background of more general laws, just as biology is impossible without the prior laws of physics and chemistry. Sociology is the foundation of psychology.

This Freud has failed to see. To him all mental phenomena are simply the interaction and mutual distortion of the instincts, of which culture and social organisations are a projection, and yet this social environment, produced by the instincts, is just what tortures and inhibits the instincts. Freud is powerless to explain causally the intricate and rich movement of cultural development, because he is in the position of a man trying to lift himself off the ground by his bootlaces. All this rich culture, its art, its science, and its institutions, is to Freud merely a projection of man's instinctive turmoil into unchanging reality, and yet this projection continually changes, although the individual instincts and reality remain the same. Why do social relations change? Why do psyches alter from age to age? Freud, like all modern psychologists who base themselves on the unchanging instincts of the genotype, is powerless to explain the only thing that interests psychology, the thing that *constitutes* psychology, the perpetual variation and development of the mental phenotype. Like Plato's men in the cave, psychoanalysts try to deduce from shadows what is happening outside. Looking into the psyche, they are mystified by the movements caused by currents in outer reality and mistake them for the distortions of the cunning and oppressed instincts, or for the interventions of mysterious 'forces' that are generated by the instincts. Seeing the shadows make a circular detour round one place, they assume this to be an eternal law of the psyche, the Oedipus complex. It does not occur to them that it may be due to an obstacle in the environment, round which the shadows have to move, and that the complex will alter if the obstacle is moved.

Unable to see psychology causally simply because they cannot see it sociologically, Freudism can attain to no psychology beyond bourgeois psychology. They never advance beyond the view-point of the 'individual in civil society'. Whether they study primitive man or lay down general laws of the soul, it is always with ideas formulated from a bourgeois psyche studying other bourgeois psyches, and so the instincts play always the part of splendid and free brutes, crippled by the repressions of a cruel culture. It is true that to-day the system of production relations is crippling man's splendid powers, but Freudian 'libido' in bondage to repression is a very inadequate myth to convey this reality. It is a pale subjective 'reflection' of the vital objective situation. The old bourgeois symbol of 'original sin' is better. The psyche, a creation of its environment, becomes to Freud, who ignores the environment or is ignorant of its mode of change, a creature whom mysterious self-generated entities force to become an unhappy bourgeois psyche. It is as if a man, seeing a row of trees bent in various ways by the prevailing winds, were without studying the relation between growth and environment to deduce that a mysterious complex in trees caused them always to lean as the result of a death instinct attracting them to the ground, while eternal Eros bade them spring up vertically. Freud's error is so much the worse because the psyche, studied by psychology, is far more the result of environmental conditions than the whole tree. The psyche is the organ of adaptation to social relations, therefore for psychology the laws determining social relations are fundamental.

Thus Freudism, like all 'individual' psychologies, breaks down in the most elementary scientific desideratum, that of causality. Though evolved as a therapy, it turns out to be the creed of undiluted pessimism. If we do not know the laws of our environment, we cannot know ourselves, and if we cannot know ourselves, we can never be free. If we are full of bitterness, and this bitterness is the outcome of an inevitable instinctual strife, our hearts can never be sweetened. If we owe no vital part of our consciousness to our environment, it is of no value to change it. 'New skies,' said Horace, 'the exile finds, but the same heart.' If we regard the categories of the present as final, and the present is full of despair and neurosis, of slumps and wars, we can never pass beyond them to a successful issue. At the best, like the neurotic, we can only return to a former successful solution at an infantile level – to feudalism, barbarian group-leadership, *unanisme*, Fascism. Indeed Jung invokes as our only salvation this very regression, appealing to the old barbarous mythologies to come to our aid. Freud at least has the courage to spurn this way of escape, and so, like a Roman stoic, in decaying classical civilisation he treads the die-hard path, and drinks the cup of poison to its dregs.

This conception, apparently refined, of the last fatal battle of the gods, is really barbarous, and the first step in the path to Hindoo resignation and vegetable sanctity. Spengler is the prophet of this resignation to one's own limitations: 'Only dreamers believe that there is a way out. We are born in this time and must bravely follow the path to the destined end. There is no other way. Our duty is to hold on to the last position, without hope, without rescue.' Freud, too, in *The Future of an Illusion* and *Group Psychology*, sees little hope for culture. Yet he is, in spite of this, more optimistic than the Communist in that he believes that while society rushes downhill, the psychoanalyst, as an individual, can do what all society fails to do, and cure the neurotic produced by modern conditions. This contradictory belief that the individual can do what the sum of individuals, of which he is one, cannot do, is characteristic of all these bourgeois pessimists, and makes it difficult to take their pessimism as completely sincere.

It is generally believed that the relation between environment and individual is correctly expressed in Adler, exponent of Individual Psychology, and Freud's former pupil. Let us therefore hear him: 'In a civilisation where one man is the enemy of the other – for this is what our whole industrial system means – demoralisation is ineradicable, for demoralisation and crime are the by-products of the struggle for existence as known to our industrialised civilisation.'

Surely, it will be said, Adler has escaped from the bourgeois cage. Surely he has realised that it is the environment, bourgeois capitalism, that produces our present discontents, and not the struggle-for-existence of the organism, pushed on by its instincts, that produces bourgeois capitalism. True, he here confuses industrialisation (machine technique) with the competition of capitalism which gave rise to it, but is separable from it. He is confounding productive forces and productive relations. Yet, at least (it will be urged), the root of the matter is in him. Let us therefore continue the quotation and see his remedy for this 'ineradicable' demoralisation: 'To limit and do away with this demoralisation, a chair of curative pedagogy should be established.'

This is the logic of Individual Psychology! Man's demoralisation, his neurosis, his discontent, his despair, are correctly seen to be due to his environment – capitalist social relations. To cure it, however, his environment is not to be changed, for the environment is always in all bourgeois economics and sociology and in spite of history presumed to be unchangeable. Rather, man is to lift himself off the ground by his bootlaces; to take pedagogic pills to cure the earthquake of capitalism's collapse. The pill takes various forms: it is a chair of curative pedagogy with Adler. With Freud the sufferers, if rich enough, are to go to an analyst for a course of treatment. This is impracticable, Jung realises, for the poorer classes, so we must re-introduce the old myths, of the archetypal hero swallowed by the giant fish ('Psychology of the Unconscious'.) These are the doctors who stand by the bedside of society in its most gigantic agony! Is it surprising that the criticism of the Marxist sometimes contains a tinge of contempt?

The Marxian has been often reproached for his antagonism to psycho-analysis. It is even asserted that the founder, it is said, has no bourgeois illusions; he is a thoroughgoing materialist. But he is not. Freud is still possessed by the focal bourgeois illusion, that the individual stands opposed to an unchanging society which trammels him, and within whose constraints his instincts attempt freely to develop the rich and varied phenomena of the psyche. Because of that illusion, Freud thinks society itself is doomed to frustration, and yet thinks that one individual can cure another. He is never able to see that just as man must have a fulcrum outside him to lift himself, so the individual must act on the environment which created his consciousness in order to change it. We owe much to Freud for his symbolic presentation of the discord between the deep and recent layers of men's minds; but he cannot heal us, for he cannot even teach us that first truth, that we must change the world in order to change ourselves.

The revolt of all the instincts against current social relations, which to Freud is everything and obscures his whole horizon, so that he writes all psychology, art, religion, culture, politics and history in terms of this revolt, is only one of many signals to the Marxian that, behind the decayed façade, a new environment is being realised and in man's troubled soul a wider consciousness, too, awaits delivery.

3

Liberty: A Study in Bourgeois Illusion

[NB: This selection begins at the mid-point of Caudwell's essay.]

Implicit in the conception of thinkers like Russell and Forster, that all social relations are restraints on spontaneous liberty, is the assumption that the animal is the only completely free creature. No one constrains the solitary carnivore to do anything. This is of course an ancient fallacy. Rousseau is the famous exponent. Man is born free but is everywhere in chains. Always in the bourgeois mind is this legend of a golden age, of a perfectly good man corrupted by institutions. Unfortunately, not only is man not good without institutions, he is not evil either. He is no man at all; he is neither good nor evil; he is an unconscious brute.

Russell's idea of liberty is the unphilosophical idea of bestiality. Narkover School is not such a bad illustration of Russell's liberty after all. [Narkover School is a reference from a 1935 film comedy dependent on self-serving anti-social behaviour.] The man alone, unconstrained, answerable only to his instincts, is Russell's free man. Thus all man's painful progress from the beasts is held to be useless. All men's work and sweat and revolutions have been away from freedom. If this is true, and if a man believes, as most of us do, as Russell does, that freedom is the essential goal of human effort, then civilisation should be abandoned and we should return to the woods. I am a Communist because I believe in freedom. I criticise Russell, and Wells, and E. M. Forster, because I believe they are the champions of unfreedom.

But this is going too far, it will be said. How can these men, who have defended freedom of thought, action, and morality, be champions of unfreedom? Let us proceed with our analysis and we shall see why.

Society is a creation by which man attains a fuller measure of freedom than the beasts. It is society and society alone, that differentiates man qualitatively from the beasts. The essential feature of society is economic production. Man, the individual, cannot do what he wants alone. He is unfree alone. Therefore he attains freedom by co-operation with his fellows. Science, by which he becomes conscious of outer reality, is social. Art, by which he becomes conscious of his feelings, is social. Economic production, by which he makes outer reality conform to his feeling, is social, and generates in its interstices science and art. It is economic production then that gives man freedom. It is because of economic production that man is free, and beasts are not. This is clear from the fact that economic production is the manipulation, by means of agriculture, horse-taming, road-building, car-construction, light, heating, and other engineering, of the environment, conformably to man's will. It enables man to do what he wills; and he can only do what he wills with the help of others. Without roads, food supplies, machines, houses, and clothes, he would be like the man in a plaster cast, who can will what he likes, and yet is not a free man but a captive. But even his free will depends on it. For consciousness develops by the evolution of language, science, and art, and these are all born of economic production. Thus the freedom of man's actions depends on his material level, on his economic production. The more advanced the economic production, the freer the civilisation.

But, it will be argued, economic production is just what entails all the 'constraints' of society. Daily work, division of labour under superintendents, all the laws of contract and capital, all the regulations of society, arise out of this work of economic production. Precisely, for, as we saw, freedom is the consciousness of causality. And by economic production, which makes it possible for man to achieve in action his will, man becomes conscious of the means *necessary* to achieve it. That a lever *must* be of a certain length to move the stone man *wills* to move is one consequence; the other is that a certain number of men *must* co-operate in a certain way to wield the lever. From this it is only a matter of development to the complicated machinery of modern life, with all its elaborate social relations.

Thus all the 'constraints', 'obligations', 'inhibitions', and 'duties' of society are the very means by which freedom is obtained by men. Liberty is thus the social consciousness of necessity. Liberty is not just necessity, for all reality is united by necessity. Liberty is the consciousness of necessity – in outer reality, in myself, and in the social relations which mediate between outer reality and human selves. The beast is a victim of mere necessity, man is in society conscious and self-determined. Not of course absolutely so, but more so than the beast.

Thus freedom of action, freedom to do what we will, the vital part of liberty, is seen to be secured by the social consciousness of necessity, and to be generated in the process of economic production. The price of liberty is not eternal vigilance, but eternal work.

But what is the relation of society to the other part of liberty, freedom to will? Economic production makes man free to do what he wills, but is he free to will what he will?

We saw that he was only free to do what he willed by attaining the consciousness of outer necessity. It is equally true that he is only free to will what he will by attaining the consciousness of inner necessity. Moreover, these two are not antagonistic, but, as we shall now find, they are one. Consciousness is the result of a specific and highly important form of economic production.

Suppose someone had performed the regrettable experiment of turning Bertrand Russell, at the age of nine months, over to a goat foster-mother, and leaving him to her care, in some remote spot, unvisited by human beings, to grow to manhood. When, say forty years later, men first visited Bertrand Russell, would they find him with the manuscripts of the *Analysis of Mind* and the *Analysis of Matter* in his hands? Would they even find him in possession of his definition of number, as the class of all classes? No. In contradiction to his present state, his behaviour would be both illogical and impolite.

It looks, therefore, as if Russell, as we know and value him, is primarily a social product. Russell is a philosopher and not an animal because he was taught not only manners, but language, and so given access to the social wisdom of ages of effort. Language filled his head with ideas, showed him what to observe, taught him logic, put all other men's wisdom at his disposal, and awoke in him affectively the elementary decencies of society – morality, justice, and liberty. Russell's consciousness, like that of all useful social objects, was a creation. It is Russell's consciousness that is distinctively him, that is what we value in him, as compared to an anthropoid ape. Society made him, just as it makes a hat.

It goes without saying that Russell's natural gifts (or, as we say more strictly, his genotype) were of importance to the outcome. But that is only to say that the material conditions the finished product. Society is well aware that it cannot make a silk purse out of a sow's ear or, except in special circumstances, a don out of a cretin. But it is also aware that out of iron ore you can make rocks, bridges, ships, or micrometers, and, out of that plastic material, man's genotype, you can make Aztecs, ancient Egyptians, Athenians, Prussians, proletarians, parsons, or public schoolboys.

It also goes almost without saying that a man is not a hat. He is a unique social product, the original of Butler's fantasy of machines that gave birth to machines. He himself is one of those machines. The essential truth about man, as compared with hats, is that he is not a hat, but the man who wears it. And the essential truth about this fashioning process of man by society, is that the fashioning is primarily of his consciousness, a process that does not take place with anything else. Now it is precisely because society elaborates his consciousness, that man, although a social product like a hat, is capable of free will, whereas a hat, being unconscious, is not capable of free will. The coming-to-be of a man, his 'growing up', is society fashioning *itself*, a group of consciousnesses, themselves made by previous consciousnesses, making another. So the torch of liberty is handed on, and burns still brighter. But it is in living that man's consciousness takes its distinctive stamp, and living is simply entering into social relations.

But, it will be urged, man – the individual – sees the world for himself alone – mountains, sky, and sea. Alone in his study he reflects on fate and death. True. But mountains and sea have a meaning to him, precisely because he is articulate-speaking, because he has a socially-moulded consciousness. Death, fate, and sea are highly-evolved social concepts. Each individual contributes a little to altering and elaborating them, but how small a contribution compared to the immense pressure of the past! Language, science, and art are all simply the results of man's uniting with his fellows socially to learn about himself and outer reality, in order to impose his desires upon it. Both knowledge and effort are only possible in co-operation, and both are made necessary by man's struggles to be freer.

Thus man's inner freedom, the conscious will, acting towards conscious ends, is a product of society; it is an economic product. It is the most refined of the products society achieves in its search for freedom. Social consciousness flowers out of social effort. We give vent in effort to our instinctive desires. Learning how to accomplish them, we learn something about the nature of reality and how to master it. This wisdom modifies the nature of our desires, which become more conscious, more full of accurate images of reality. So enriched, the desires become subtler, and, in working to achieve profounder goals, in more elaborate economic production gain still deeper insight into reality, and, as consequence, themselves become yet more enriched. Thus, in dialectic process, social being generates social mind, and this interplay between deepening inner and outer reality is conserved and passed on by culture. Man, as society advances, has a consciousness composed less and less of unmodified instinct, more and more of socially-fashioned knowledge and emotion. Man understands more and more clearly the necessities of his own being and of outer reality. He becomes increasingly more free.

The illusion that our minds are free to the extent that, like the beasts, we are unconscious of the causality of our mental states, is just what secures our unfreedom. Bourgeois society to-day clearly exhibits in practice this truth, which we have established by analysis in theory. The bourgeois believes that liberty consists in absence of social organisation; that liberty is a negative quality, a deprivation of existing obstacles to it, and not a positive quality, the reward of endeavour and wisdom. This belief is itself the outcome of bourgeois social relations. As a result of it, the bourgeois intellectual is unconscious of the causality that makes his consciousness what it is. Like the neurotic who refuses to believe that his compulsion is the result of a certain unconscious complex, the bourgeois refuses to believe that his conception of liberty as a mere deprivation of social restraints arises from bourgeois social relations themselves, and that it is just this illusion which is constraining him on every side. He refuses to see that his own limited liberty, the captivity of the worker, and all the contradictions of developing bourgeois relations – pacifism, fascism, war, hate, cruelty, disease – are bound in one net of causality, that each is influenced by each, and that therefore it is fallacious to suppose a simple effort of the will of the free man, without knowledge of the causes, will banish fascism, war, and slumps. Because of his basic fallacy, this type of intellectual always tries to cure positive social evils, such as wars, by negative individual actions, such as non-co-operation, passive resistance or conscientious objection. This is because he cannot rid himself of the assumption that the individual is free. But we have shown that the individual is never free. He can only attain freedom by social co-operation. He can only do what he wants by using social forces. If, therefore, he wishes to stop poverty, war, and misery, he must do it, not by passive resistance, but by using social relations. But in order to use social relations, he must understand them. He must become conscious of the laws of society, just as, if he wants to lever up a stone, he must know the laws of levers.

Once the bourgeois intellectual can see that society is the only instrument of freedom, he has advanced a step farther along the road to freedom. But until then he is unfree. True, he is a logician, he understands the causality of nature, Einstein's theories, all the splendid apparatus of social discovery, but he still believes in a magic world of social relations divorced from these theories, in which only the god of bourgeois liberty rules. This is proved, not only in his theory, in the way his doctrine of liberty is accepted like a theological dogma, and never made to square with all his philosophic and scientific knowledge; but it is also proved in action, when the bourgeois intellectual is powerless to stop the development of increasing unfreedom in bourgeois society. All the compulsions of militancy, fascism, and economic distress harry contemporary society, and all he can oppose to them is individualistic action, conscientious objection and passive resistance. This is bound to be the case if he is unfree. Like a man who believes he can walk upon the water and drowns in it, the bourgeois intellectual asserts a measure of freedom that does not in fact exist, and is therefore unfree mentally and physically. Who cannot see iron compulsion stalking through the bourgeois world today? We are free when we can do what we will. Society is an instrument of freedom in so far as it secures what men want. The members of bourgeois society, all of them, worker, capitalist, and capitalist-intellectual, want an increase in material wealth, happiness, freedom from strife, from danger of death, security. But bourgeois society to-day produces a decrease in material wealth and also creates unemployment, unhappiness, strife, insecurity, constant war. Therefore all who live in bourgeois society – democratic, fascist or Rooseveltian – are unfree, for bourgeois society is not giving them what they desire. The fact that they have, or have not, votes or 'freedom of speech' does not alter, in any way, their unfreedom.

Why does not bourgeois society fulfil the wants of its members? Because it does not understand the laws of economic production – it is unorganised and unplanned. It is unconscious of the necessities of economic production, and, because of that, cannot make economic production fulfil its desires. Why is it unconscious of the necessities of economic production? Because, for historical reasons, it believes that economic production is best when each man is left free to produce for himself what seems to him most profitable to produce. In other words, it believes that freedom is secured by the lack of social organisation of the individual in the function of society, economic production. As we saw, this individual freedom through unconsciousness is a delusion. Unconscious, deluded bourgeois society is therefore unfree. Even Russell is unfree, and in the next war, as in the last, will be put in gaol.

This very unfreedom – expressed as individualism – in the basic function of society, ultimately generates every form of external constraint. The bourgeois revolutionary asserted a fallacious liberty – that man was born good and was everywhere in chains, that institutions made him bad. It turned out that this liberty he claimed was individualism in private production. This revealed its fallacious nature as a freedom by appearing at once as a restraint. For it could only be secured, it was only a name, for unrestricted right to own the means of production, which is in itself a restriction on those who are thus alienated from their livelihood. Obviously, what I own absolutely my neighbour is restricted from touching.

All social relations based on duty and privilege were changed by the bourgeois revolution into exclusive and forcible rights to ownership of cash. I produce for my individual self, for profit. Necessarily, therefore, I produce for the market, not for use. I work for cash, not from duty to my lord or retainer. My duties to the State could all now be compounded for cash. All my obligations of contract, whether of marriage or social organisation, could be compounded for cash. Cash appeared as the only obligation between men and men, who were otherwise apparently completely free – free master, free labourer, free producer, free consumer, free markets, free trade, free entrepreneur, the free flow of capital from hand to hand and land to land. And even man's obligations to cash appeared an obligation of cash to him, to be absolutely owned by him.

This dissolution of social obligations could be justified if man was free in himself, and if, doing what seemed best for him, for his own good and profit, he would in fact get what he desired, and so secure freedom. It was a return to the apparent liberty of the jungle, where each beast struggles only for himself, and owes no obligations to anyone. But this liberty, as we saw, is an illusion. The beast is less free than man. The desires of the jungle cancel each other out, and no one gets exactly what he wants. No beast is free.

This fallacy at once revealed itself as a fallacy in the following way. Complete freedom to own property meant that society found itself divided into haves and have-nots, like the beasts in the jungle. The have-nots, each trying to do what was best for him in the given circumstances, according to the bourgeois doctrine of liberty, would have forcibly seized the property from the haves. But this would have been complete anarchy, and though anarchy, according to bourgeois theory, is complete liberty, in practice the bourgeois speedily sees that to live in the jungle is not to be free. Property is the basis of his mode of living. In such circumstances, social production could not be carried on, and society would dissolve, man return to savagery, and freedom altogether perish. Thus the bourgeois contradicted his theory in practice from the start. The State took its distinctive modern form as the enforcement of bourgeois rights by coercion. Police, standing army and laws were all brought into being to protect the haves from the 'free' desires of the have-nots. Bourgeois liberty at once gives rise to bourgeois coercion, to prisons, armies, contracts, to all the sticky and restraining apparatus of the law, to all the ideology and education centred round the sanctity of private property, to all the bourgeois commandments. Thus bourgeois liberty was built on a lie, bound to reveal in time its contradictions.

Among the have-nots, bourgeois freedom gave rise to fresh coercions. The free labourer, owning nothing, was free to sell his labour in any market. But this became a form of slavery worse, in its unrestricted form, than chattel slavery, a horror that Government Blue Books describing pre-Factory Act conditions make vivid for all their arid phraseology. They show how unrestricted factory industrialisation made beasts of men, women, and children, how they died of old age in their thirties, how they rose early in the morning exhausted to work and knocked off late at night only to sink exhausted to sleep, how the children were aged by work before they had ceased to be infants. Made worse than a slave – for he was still free to be unemployed – the labourer fought for freedom by enforcing social restraints on his employers. Banding with others in trade unions, he began the long fight that gave rise to the various Factory Acts, wage agreements, and all the elaborate social legislation which to-day coerces the bourgeois employer.

And, after all this, even the bourgeois himself is not free. The unrestricted following of his illusion of liberty enslaves him. His creed demands unrestricted competition, and this, because it is unrestricted, works as wildly and blindly as the weather. It makes him as unfree, as much at the mercy of a not understood chance, as a cork bobbing on the waves. So he too seeks freedom in restraint – industry is increasingly sheltered by amalgamations, rings, tariffs, price agreements, 'unfair competition' clauses, subsidies, and Government protection for the exploitation of Colonial areas. Bourgeois liberty makes overt its self-contradictions by becoming monopoly.

Here is the secret paradox of bourgeois development and decline. The bourgeois abandoned feudal relations in the name of a liberty which he visualised as freedom from social restraints. Such a liberty would have led to savagery. But in fact the liberty he claimed – 'unrestricted' private property – really involved restraint, that is, it gave rise to complex forms of social organisation, which were more many-sided, more incessant, and more all-pervading, than feudal restraints. Thus the cash relation, which he conceived as putting an end to all social restraints, and thus giving him liberty, did give him a larger measure of liberty than in feudalism, but in the opposite way to his expectations, by imposing far more complex organisations than those of feudal civilisation. All the elaborate forms of bourgeois contracts, market organisation, industrial structure, national States, trade unions, tariffs, Imperialism, and bureaucratic democratic government, the iron pressure of the consumer and the labour market, the dole, subsidy, bounties – all these multifarious forms of social organisation – were brought into being by a class that demanded the dissolution of social organisation. And the fact that bourgeois civilisation obtained a greater measure of control over its environment than feudal – and was that much freer – is precisely because all these complex social organisations were brought into being – but brought blindly.

Blindly brought into being, that is the source of the ultimate unfreedom of bourgeois civilisation. Because it is not conscious of the fact that private ownership of the means of production, unrestricted competition, and the cash nexus of their natures, involve various forms of restraint – alienation from property, captivity to slump and war, unemployment and misery – bourgeois society is unable to control itself. The various forms of social organisation it has blindly erected, as an animal tunnelling for gold might throw up great mounds of earth, are all haphazard and not understood. It believes that to become conscious of them fully, to manipulate them consciously for the ends of the will, is to be an advocate of determinism, to kill liberty, to bring into birth the bee-hive state. For still, in spite of all the havoc the bourgeois sees around him, he believes that only the beast is free, and that to be subject to all the winds of chance, at the mercy of wars and slumps and social strife, is to be free.

Any definition of liberty is humbug that does not mean this: liberty to do what one wants. A people is free whose members have liberty to do what they want – to get the goods they desire and avoid the ills they hate. What do men want? They want to be happy, and not to be starved or despised or deprived of the decencies of life. They want to be secure, and friendly with their fellows, and not conscripted to slaughter and be slaughtered. They want to marry, and beget children, and help, not oppress each other. Who is free who cannot do these things, even if he has a vote, and free speech? Who then is free in bourgeois society, for not a few men but millions are forced by circumstances to be unemployed, and miserable, and despised, and unable to enjoy the decencies of life? Millions are forced to go out and be slaughtered, or to kill, and to oppress each other. Millions are forced to strive with their fellows for a few glittering prizes, and to be deprived of marriage, and a home, and children, because society cannot afford them these things. Millions and millions of men are not free. These are the elements of liberty, and it is insane – until these are achieved – for a limited class to believe it can secure the subtleties of liberty. Only when these necessities are achieved, can man rise higher and, by the practice of art and science, learn more clearly what he wants, and what he can get, having only then passed from the sphere of necessity to that of freedom.

Each step to higher consciousness is made actively with struggle and difficulty. It is man's natural but fatal error to suppose that the path of liberty is easy, that it is a mere negative, a relaxation, the elimination of an obstacle in his path. But it is more than that. True freedom must be created as strenuously as we make the instruments of freedom, tools, and machines. It must be wrested out of the heart of reality, including the inner reality of man's mind.

That is why all lovers of liberty, who have understood the nature of freedom, and escaped from the ignorant categories of bourgeois thought, turn to Communism. For that is simply what Communism is, the attainment of more liberty than bourgeois society can reach. Communism has as its basis the understanding of the causality of society, so that all the unfreedom involved in bourgeois society, the enslavement of the have-nots by the haves, and the slavery of both haves and have-nots to wars, slumps, depression, and superstition, may be ended. To be conscious of the laws of dead matter: that is something; but it is not enough. Communism seizes hold of a higher degree of self-determination, to rescue man from war, starvation, hate, and coercion, by becoming conscious of the causality of society. It is Communism that makes free will real to man, by making society conscious of itself. To change reality we must understand its laws. If we *wish* to move a stone, we *must* apply the leverage in the proper place. If we *wish* to change bourgeois social relations into communist, we *must* follow a certain path. The have-nots, the proletariat, must take over the means of production from the haves, the bourgeoisie, and since, as we saw, these two freedoms are incompatible, restraint, in the form of the coercive state, must remain in being as long as the bourgeoisie try to get back their former property. But, unlike the former situation, this stage is only temporary. This stage is what is known as the dictatorship of the proletariat, the necessary step from the dictatorship of the bourgeoisie – which is what the bourgeois state is – to the classless State, which is what Communism is. And as Russia shows, even in the dictatorship of the proletariat, before the classless State has come into being, man is already freer. He can avoid unemployment, and competition with his fellows, and poverty. He can marry and beget children, and achieve the decencies of life. He is not asked to oppress his fellows.

To the worker, subject to unemployment, starved in the midst of plenty, this path eventually becomes plain. Despite the assurances of the bourgeoisie that in a democratic or national State he is completely free, he revolts. And who, in those days, will stand by his side? Will the bourgeoisie, themselves pinched and disfranchised by the growing concentration of capital, discouraged, pessimistic, harried into war and oppression by 'forces beyond control', and yet still demanding liberty? On the answer to that question, which each individual bourgeois must make, sooner or later, will depend whether he strives in those days to make men free or to keep them in chains. And this too depends on whether he has understood the nature of liberty. The class to whom capitalism means liberty steadily contracts, but those once of that class who are now enslaved to war, imperialism, and poverty, still cling to that bourgeois interpretation of liberty that has abundantly proved its falsehood. They can only escape and become free by understanding the active nature of liberty, and by becoming conscious of the path they must follow to attain it. Their will is not free as long as they will liberty but produce unfreedom. It is only free when they will communism and produce liberty.

This good, liberty, contains all good. Not only at the simple level of current material wants, but where all men's aspirations bud, freedom is the same goal, pursued in the same way. Science is the means by which man learns what he can do, and therefore it explores the necessity of outer reality. Art is the means by which man learns what he wants to do, and therefore it explores the essence of the human heart. And bourgeoisdom, shutting its eyes to beauty, turning its back on science, only follows its stupidity to the end. It crucifies liberty upon a cross of gold, and if you ask in whose name it does this, it replies, 'In the name of personal freedom'.

PART II

Illusion and Reality

Illusion and Reality is Caudwell's most innovative and most complete work. It was published by Macmillan, not a radical publisher, in 1937. Lawrence & Wishart, the Communist Party publisher, put out a new edition in 1946, and reprinted in 1947, 1950, 1955, 1958 and 1966, with a new edition in 1973, reprinted in 1977 (the edition used for this collection). In the biographical note to the 1946 edition, it was heralded as the 'first comprehensive attempt to work out a Marxist theory of art'.[9] Caudwell begins the book by rejecting the common assumption that 'literature can be completely criticised in terms of literature.' He stresses that he is writing about the sources of poetry, which 'cannot be separated from the study of society'. Poetry is social. It is socially transmitted, it has a social content and – in what most distinguishes Caudwell's argument – it has a social purpose. Most other Marxist treatments of literature were 'reflectionist', treating literature as reflecting the social relationships of the age; Caudwell saw it not only as reflective but, most importantly, as active and performing a social function.

At the most general level, literature and art were guides to action, guiding in the sense of organising emotional responses and clarifying the values that underlie choices rather than presenting information. Caudwell has been criticised for approaching literature in this way, not just because he makes political judgements but because he doesn't follow the traditional literary critical practice of analysing specific works in detail. Rather, he is concerned primarily with the social structures that shape people's thinking and how literature relates to that process. At one point, he defined himself as a social rather than a literary critic. For students of literature, who may sometimes question the social value of what they are studying, especially if they have been accused of being self-indulgent dilettantes, Caudwell deals with questions of more obvious social importance like 'why is there literature?' and 'does it have any material value?' He shows that literature over the ages has had and still has an important social task; it is that perspective from which he criticises it.

Because he was writing more than eighty years ago, it is useful to recognise certain aspects of linguistic change. Caudwell regularly refers to the undifferentiated individual as 'he', customary in most writing until a couple of decades ago, but his crime writing shows him to be very much aware of sexism and displays his anti-sexist attitudes. His use of 'phantasy' and 'phantastic' is not the choice of a pretentious spelling variant but, as used in some writing of the early twentieth century, draws on an aspect of the Greek root that stresses the visual (think of 'phantom'). He also uses the word 'economic' rather loosely, extending its range to activity whose importance is economic even though it may not be strictly regarded itself as economic. It is also important to note that his reading in anthropology was in books that might well have been written a century ago, with assumptions that are questionable today.

For readers who have read the *Studies*, using 'bourgeois' as a positive term may seem strange for Caudwell. But the Communist revolutionary Caudwell admired the bourgeoisie as historically revolutionary: '... at every step the bourgeois is revolutionary in that he revolutionises his own basis. But he revises it only to make it consistently more bourgeois' (*IR*, p. 103) – which, in Caudwell's optimistic eyes, will soon lead to 'the final conflict' of the proletarian revolution.

I have made selections from his Chapters 1–6 and Chapter 8. They deal, at first, with poetry's function in pre-industrial tribal society and then trace the development of English poetry in relation to the changing economic structure. He shows how poetry reflects the consciousness conditioned by the economic base and also consolidates social outlook. I have included the table that presents the historical development of English poetry, which, because it is compact, has the value of a historical view that can be taken in all at once, although it has been much criticised as crude. This criticism is fair but the problem is in part attributable to it being so condensed.

Chapter 8 explains how language mechanisms work in shaping individual emotional responses to poetry. Its importance is the sense of how concrete experience of poetry can actually have a social function. And it also shows Caudwell's moving towards considering the contemporary literary scene in terms of revolution.

The following chapters I have not included: Chapter 7 is more specialised, defining the characteristics of poetry, and Chapters 9–11 move to a somewhat different subject matter – psychology and the arts, the distinction between dream and poetic 'phantasy', the relation between the different arts and between the arts and science. The final chapter, discussed in the general introduction, is explicitly political; Caudwell says that only with a revolution can literature regain its proper functioning.

Please note that I have not retained the numbers of the section divisions; when such divisions occur within the quoted text, they are indicated by extra space. Omissions from the text are indicated by ellipses or three asterisks for larger ones. To avoid a profusion of ellipses, I have not indicated when material begins or ends mid-paragraph.

4

The Birth of Poetry

* * *

Poetry, maid-of-all-work in a simple tribal economy, becomes in the rich elaboration of a modern culture an activity which exists side by side with the novel, history and the drama. This development will give us the clue, not merely to the meaning of poetry, but also, if we follow the successive trails as they open up, to the significance in man's life of all art and science.

* * *

The non-biological change of man, superimposed upon his relatively constant biological make-up during historic times, is the subject of literary history. This development is non-biological just because it is economic. It is the story of man's struggle with Nature, in which his increasing mastery of her and himself is due, not to any improvement in his inborn qualities but to improvements in systems of production, including tools, the technique of using them, language, social systems, houses, and other transmissible external structures and relations. This inheritance is the vast concrete accumulation of 'human qualities' which are not transmitted somatically but socially. Mother wit is needed for their use, but it is a plastic force which inflates these developing and transmitted forms. Looked at in this way, culture cannot be separated from economic production or poetry from social organisation. They stand together in sharp opposition to the ordinary biological properties of species.

Poetry is to be regarded then, not as anything racial, national, genetic or specific in its essence, but as something economic.

* * *

Individual differences are genetic, the result of a particular pack of genes. Biologically speaking, they are 'variations'. But social differentiation means that an individual plays a particular role in social production. This differentiation may be the very antithesis of individuation, for by it the individual may be pressed into a mould – whether that of miner, bank clerk, lawyer, or parson – which is bound to suppress some part of his native individuality. He becomes a *type* instead of an individual. An inherited character is forced into an acquired mould. The greater the differentiation, the more specialised will be the mould and the more painful the adjustment. Psychologically, as Jung has shown, the process takes place by the exaltation of one psychic function – that most marked genetically, and therefore most likely to prove economically remunerative. The hypertrophy of this function and its accommodation to the purposes of the chosen professional type result in the wilting of the other psychic functions, which eventually become largely unconscious, and in the unconscious exercise an opposing force to the conscious personality. Hence the typical 'modern' unease and neuroses. Twentieth-century civilisation, the creation of a gospel of unadulterated economic individualism, has thus finally become anti-individualistic. It opposes the full development of genetic possibilities by forcing the individual to mould a favoured function along the lines of a type whose services possess exchange-value; so that for a refreshing contrast we turn (like T. E. Lawrence) to a nomad civilisation such as that of the Bedouins. Here genetic individuality, the character of a man, is most respected and most highly developed; and yet it is just here that economic differentiation is at a minimum.

Does this mean that biological individuality is opposed to economic differentiation, and that civilisation fetters the 'free' instincts – as the followers of Freud, Adler, Jung, and D. H. Lawrence by implication claim? No, it is precisely economic differentiation, by the possibility of specialisation that it affords, which gives opportunity for the most elaborate development of the peculiarities or 'variations' constituting the 'difference' of a biological individual. But this opportunity presupposes a free choice by any individual of the complete range of economic functions. There is no such free choice in modern civilisation, because of its class structure. Not only is an individual heavily weighted in the direction of following an occupation approximately equivalent in income and cost of training to that of his parents, but also a marked bent for a slightly remunerative occupation (such as poetry) will be sacrificed to a slight bent for a markedly remunerative occupation (such as company promoting), while the career of being unemployed, the involuntary function of so many millions today, muffles all useful variations.

It is not civilisation as such which by its differentiation stifles genetic individuality; on the contrary, its complexity gives added scope for its development and increases the sum of 'standard deviation'. One incident of civilisation – the development of classes in society and the increasing restriction of choice of function for the individual – holds back the very development of individuality which the existing productive forces could allow in a more fluid system of social relations. Capitalism, by making all talents and gifts a commodity subject to the inexorable and iron laws of the 'free' market, now restrains that free development of the individual which its vast productive forces could easily permit, if released. This gives rise to the complaints of the instincts tortured by civilisation which are investigated by Freud, Jung, and Adler.

*   *   *

Durkheim's conception of a tribe whose consciousness is solid crystal and undifferentiated, corresponding to its undifferentiated economy, in its absoluteness misses the significance of genetic individuality as the basis of economic differentiation, just as the conception of the instincts of civilised man fighting the constraints of society ignores the importance of economic differentiation as a fruitful outlet for individuality. Biologists will notice here a significant parallel to the famous dispute on their own science over 'acquired' and 'innate' characters.

Durkheim distinguishes the collective representations of the tribe which constitute its collective mind, from individual representations which constitute the individual mind, because of the coercive character of the former. This error is only the fundamental error of contemporary philosophy which, by its false conception of the nature of freedom, continually generates the same stale antithesis. The consciousness made possible by the development of society is not by its nature coercive; on the contrary this consciousness, expressed in science and art, is the means whereby man attains freedom. Social consciousness, like social labour, of which it is the product and auxiliary, is the instrument of man's freedom. And it is not the instincts unadapted by society which are of their essence free; on the contrary the unmodified instincts deliver man into the slavery of blind necessity and unconscious compulsion.

Yet social consciousness is sometimes felt by men as coercive – why is this? Because it is a consciousness which no longer represents social truth; because it is no longer generated freely in the whole process of social co-operation. Such a consciousness is the product of a class antagonism; it is the consciousness of a class which by the development of the division of labour and absolute property-right has become isolated from economic production, and is therefore maimed and obsolete. This consciousness now becomes the bulwark of privilege instead of the spontaneous expression of social fact, and must therefore be coercively enforced on the rest of society. Durkheim does not see that this coercive type of group consciousness is least common with a primitive people, and most common with a sophisticated civilisation.

* * *

We call the primitive's heightened language, which is as it were speech in ceremonial dress, *poetry*, and we saw how in the course of evolution it became prosaic and branched into history, philosophy, theology, the story and drama. This raises a question whether poetry was ever anything but a reflection of the undifferentiated economy in which it was born, and whether poetry in its own right has now any real justification for existence. The fact that it still continues to exist is no complete answer, since evolution is full of vestigial organs, and poetry may be one of these. Poetry has an increasingly small 'public'. Alone in literature, it clings tenaciously to heightened language. This might be merely the stigma of degeneration, as if poetry, like a mental deficient, still babbled in a childish tongue outgrown by the rest of the family, which has had to earn its living in an adult world.

We know there is a certain accident in the survival of poetry. Men speak, tell ancient tales, repeat bits of wisdom, and this vanishes. Poetry in its heightened language survives, and therefore we think of it as 'literature', making too artificial a separation from the rest of social speech. This in turn may lead us to overlook why poetry has a heightened language, why it survives, why it has a relative changelessness and eternity.

Primitive poetry is not so much the matrix of subsequent 'literature', as one pole of it. Because of its collective and traditional nature, it is the one which survives, and leads us, who see in it the sole literature of a primitive people, to imagine a kind of golden age in which even the oracles speak the language of epics.

What is the nature of this other pole? A modern mind, surveying the primitive scene, and noticing all the vague aspirations, religious phantasies, mythological cosmologies and collective emotions collecting at the pole of rhythmical language, would be disposed to think of the other pole as the scientific pole. This would be the pole of pure statement, of collections of facts uncoloured by emotion: pedigrees, astronomical calculations, censuses and all other literary productions which aim at a strong grasp of simple reality.

But science is not likely to seem the opposite of poetry to the primitive mind. He does not know of science as a branch of literature. He knows science only as a practice, a technique, a way of building boats and planting trees which can best and most easily be learned through a kind of dumb imitation, because the practice is common to all the members of a tribe. The idea of a statement devoid of prejudice and intended only to be the cold vehicle of sheer reality is quite alien to that mind. Words represent power, almost magical power, and the cold statement seems to divest them of this power and substitute a mirror-image of external reality. But what difference, save of inferiority, is there between the real object and its mirror-image? The image of reality which the primitive seeks in words is of a different kind: it is a magic *puppet image*, such as one makes of one's enemies. By operating on it, one operates on reality.

* * *

The function of non-rhythmical language, then, was to persuade. Born as a personal function, an extension of one individual volition, it can be contrasted with the collective spirit of rhythmical language, which draws in primitive society all its power from its collective appearance. Poetry's very rhythm makes its group celebration more easy, as for example in an infants' class, which imposes prosody upon the multiplication table it recites, making mathematics poetical.

As with all polar opposites the two interpenetrate, but on the whole the non-rhythmical language, based on everyday speech, is the language of private persuasion, and rhythmical language, the language of collective speech, is the language of public emotion. This is the most important difference in language at the level of primitive culture.

* * *

Poetry is characteristically song, and song is characteristically something which, because of its rhythm, is sung in *unison*, is capable of being the expression of a collective emotion. This is one of the secrets of 'heightened' language.

But why should the tribe *need* a collective emotion? The approach of a tiger, of a foe, of rain, of an earthquake will instinctively elicit a conditioned and collective response. All will be menaced, all will fear. Any instrument to produce such a collective emotion is therefore unnecessary in such situations. The tribe responds dumbly, like a frightened herd of deer.

But such an instrument is socially necessary when no visible or tangible cause exists, and yet such a cause is *potential*. This is how poetry grows out of the economic life of a tribe, and how illusion grows out of reality.

Unlike the life of beasts, the life of the simplest tribe requires a series of efforts which are not instinctive, but which are demanded by the necessities of a non-biological economic aim – for example, a harvest. Hence the instincts must be harnessed to the needs of the harvest by a social mechanism. An important part of this mechanism is the group festival, the matrix of poetry, which frees the stores of emotion and canalises them in a collective channel. The real object, the tangible aim – a harvest – becomes in the festival a phantastic object. The real object is not here now. The phantastic object is here now – in phantasy. As man by the violence of the dance, the screams of the music and the hypnotic rhythm of the verse is alienated from present reality, which does not contain the unsown harvest, so he is projected into the phantastic world in which these things phantastically exist. That world becomes more real, and even when the music dies away the ungrown harvest has a greater reality for him, spurring him on to the labours necessary for its accomplishment.

Thus poetry, combined with dance, ritual, and music, becomes the great switchboard of the instinctive energy of the tribe, directing it into trains of collective actions whose immediate causes or gratifications are not in the visual field and which are not automatically decided by instinct.

It is necessary to prepare the ground for harvest. It is necessary to set out on an expedition of war. It is necessary to retrench and retract in the long scarcity of winter. These collective obligations demand from man the service of his instinctive energy, yet there is no instinct which tells him to give them. Ants and bees store instinctively; but man does not. Beavers construct instinctively, not man. It is necessary to harness man's instincts to the mill of labour, to collect his emotions and direct them into the useful, the economic channel. Just because it is economic, i.e. non-instinctive, this instinct must be *directed*. The instrument which directs them is therefore economic in origin.

How can these emotions be collected? Words, in ordinary social life, have acquired emotional associations for each man. These words are carefully selected, and the rhythmical arrangement makes it possible to chant them in unison, and release their emotional associations in all the vividness of collective existence. Music and the dance cooperate to produce an alienation from reality which drives on the whole machine of society. Between the moments when the emotion is generated and raised to a level where it can produce 'work', it does not disappear. The tribal individual is changed by having participated in the collective illusion. He is educated – i.e. adapted to tribal life. The feasts or corroborees are crises of adaptation – some general and intended to last throughout life, such as the initiation or marriage ceremonies, others regularly renewed or directed to special ends, such as the harvest and war festivals or mid-winter Saturnalias.

But this collective emotion organised by art at the tribal festival, because it sweetens work and is generated by the needs of labour, goes out again into labour to lighten it. The primitive conducts such collective tasks as hoeing, paddling, ploughing, reaping, and hauling to a rhythmic chant which has an artistic content related to the needs of the task, and expressing the collective emotion behind the task.

The increasing division of labour, which includes also its increasing organisation, seems to produce a movement of poetry away from concrete living, so that art appears to be in opposition to work, a creation of leisure. The poet is typically now the solitary individual; his expression, the lyric. The division of labour has led to a class society, in which consciousness has gathered at the pole of the ruling class, whose rule eventually produces the conditions for idleness. Hence art ultimately is completely separated from work, with disastrous results to both, which can only be healed by the ending of classes. But meanwhile the movement has given rise to a rich development of technique.

These emotions, generated collectively, persist in solitude so that one man, alone, singing a song, still feels his emotion stirred by collective images. He is already exhibiting that paradox of art – man withdrawing from his fellows into the world of art, only to enter more closely into communion with humanity. Once made fluid, this collective emotion of poetic art can pervade the most individual and private transactions. Sexual love, spring, a sunset, the song of the nightingale, and the ancient freshness of the rose are enriched by all the complex history of emotions and experience shared in common by a thousand generations. None of these reactions is instinctive, therefore none is personal. To the monkey, or the man reared like Mowgli by a wolfish foster-mother, the rose would be something perhaps edible, a bright colour. To the poet it is the rose of Keats, of Anacreon, of Hafiz, of Ovid, and of Jules Laforgue. For this world of art is the world of social emotion – of words and images which have gathered, as a result of the life experiences of all, emotional associations common to all, and its increasing complexity reflects the increasing elaboration of social life.

The emotions common to all change with the development of society. The primitive food-gathering or hunting tribe projects himself into Nature to find there his own desires. He changes himself socially to conform with Nature. Hence his art is naturalistic and perceptive. It is the vivid drawing of Palaeolithic man or the bird- and animal-mimicking dances and songs of the Australian aborigine. Its sign is the totem – the man really Nature. Its religion is mana.

The crop-raising and herd-rearing tribe is an advance on this. It takes Nature into itself and changes Nature to conform, with its own desires by domestication and taming. Its art is conventional and conative. It is the arbitrary decoration of Neolithic man or the elaborate rituals of African or Polynesian tribes. Its sign is the corn-god or the beast-god – Nature really man. Its religion is one of fetishes and spirits.

The introduction of Nature into the tribe leads to a division of labour and so to the formation of chiefs, priests and ruling classes. The choragus detaches himself from the ritual and becomes an actor – an individual. The art depicts noble persons as well as gods. The chorus becomes an epic – a collective tale about individuals – and, finally, the lyric – an individual utterance. Man, already conscious, first of his difference, and then of his unity with Nature, now becomes conscious of his internal differences, because for the first time conditions exist for their realisation.

Thus the developing complex of society, in its struggle with the environment, secretes poetry as it secretes the technique of harvest, as part of its non-biological and specifically human adaptation to existence. The tool adapts the hand to a new function, without changing the inherited shape of the hands of humanity. The poem adapts the heart to a new purpose, without changing the eternal desires of men's hearts. It does so by projecting man into a world of phantasy which is superior to his present reality precisely because it is a world of superior reality – a world of more important reality not yet realised, whose realisation demands the very poetry which phantastically anticipates it. Here is room for every error, for the poem proposes something whose very reason for poetical treatment is that we cannot touch, smell or taste it yet. But only by means of the illusion can be brought into being a reality which would not otherwise exist. Without the ceremony phantastically portraying the granaries bursting with grain, the pleasures and delights of harvest, men would not face the hard labour necessary to bring it into being. Sweetened with a harvest song, the work goes well. Just because poetry is what it is, it exhibits a reality beyond the reality it brings to birth and nominally portrays, a reality which though secondary is yet higher and more complex. For poetry describes and expresses not so much the grain in its concreteness, the harvest in its factual essence – which it helps to realise and which are the conditions for its own existence – but the emotional, social, and collective complex which is that tribe's relation to the harvest. It expresses a whole new world of truth – its emotion, its comradeship, its sweat, its long-drawn-out wait, and happy consummation – which has been brought into being by the fact that man's relation to the harvest is not instinctive and blind but economic and conscious. Not poetry's abstract statement – its content of facts – but its dynamic role in society – its content of collective emotion – is therefore poetry's *truth*.

5

The Death of Mythology

* * *

Poetry is the nascent self-consciousness of man, not as an individual but as sharer with others of a whole world of common emotion. This emotion, because it is common, has for each individual an objective, and therefore pseudo-external existence. This social objectivity is confused by primitive man with material objectivity, so that the phantastic world, because it is presented to the individual 'from outside' by outside manipulation, is confused with the material world against which he bumps himself. Other men confirm by their actions the objectivity of a material world; similarly they seem to confirm a like reality for the phantastic world whose sanctions they recognise.

Man's emotions are fluid and confusing. They are projected into the outside world in animism, orondism and mana at his primitive stage of culture, not because he is one with his environment, but because he has consciously separated himself from it in order to seek his desires in it by hunting or crop-gathering. Because the environment is already something consciously distinct from himself, he is concerned with locating 'things' out there or in himself. Because these collective emotions, unlike a pain or a wound but like a sunset or a thunderstorm, are manifestly experienced by all, they gain the sanction of objectivity and therefore of material reality and are located 'out there', in the object which arouses them. Man enters into nature: nature becomes 'animated' – endowed with man's subjective soul.

What in fact is this emotional complex of tribal poetry? Is it material reality or completely ideal illusion? It is neither. It is a *social* reality. It expresses the social relation of man's instincts to the ungathered fruit. These instincts have generated these emotions just because they have not blindly followed the necessities of the germ plasm, but have been moulded by the objective necessities of collective action to a common economic end. The phantasy of poetry is a social image.

Therefore the phantastic world of poetic ritual, myth, or drama expresses a social truth, a truth about the instincts of man as they fare, not in biological or individual experience, but in associated experience. Such truths are necessarily phrased therefore in the language of the emotions. A pianola roll is pierced with holes. Those holes are real concrete entities. But they are not the music. The music is what happens when it is played. The poem is what happens when it is read.

Hence tribal poetry, and that part of religion from which it is at first indistinguishable, is man's confused knowledge of society and of his relation to it.

And magic? Man, conscious of his personal emotions, locates the irregularity in the object which stimulates them, because such conscious affects as terror and desire are due to the common experience of a tribe, are impressions common to all individuals of the tribe in relation to certain things. The emotion then seems located in these things and, because of its immediate vividness, seems the soul, the essential reality of these things. Force, the kinaesthetic sensation of muscular effort, even up to a late date dominated the thought of science, and yet expresses this primitive animistic way of regarding nature.

Man's emotions are also in him. They therefore seem under his control. They therefore seem to be the means whereby he can dominate reality – through the emotional essence of things. He, the individual, can dominate reality by his will. By evoking – through charms, ceremonies and sympathetic magic – the emotions proper to the achieved act, he believes the act accomplished. It seems to him that he can control outer reality by returning into himself. So indeed he can, but only if this thought is scientific thought and, acting as a guide to action, returns out again to grapple with reality.

Because society stands as *environment* to individual man, and as *associated men* to the environment, magic and religion overlap, and blend more closely in a primitive economy, where society is only slightly developed and is therefore a thin blanket between the individual and outer reality.

Magic gives birth to science, for magic commands outer reality to conform to certain laws, and reality refuses, so that knowledge of the stubborn nature of reality is impressed on the magician. He does not try to walk upon the water with spells, or if he does, the spells fail. Rainmakers are not found in the desert, but in regions where rain sometimes comes. No magician makes spells for a winter harvest. Thus certain stubbornnesses in reality for which stronger spells are needed are gradually recognised; and so it becomes accepted that certain laws can only be overridden by mighty forces – by gods, by Fate, and eventually Fate dissolves into that very decree that these forces may not be overborne by anyone. Even Jove is subject to Fate. Fate is law. Magic has turned into its opposite, scientific determinism.

In proportion, as man, by the development of economics, discovers more and more of the nature of reality, magic sets itself bolder and more elaborate tasks, and more and more is corrected by experience. It proposes to man phantastic possibilities, which man realises. But he does not realise them by magic. Without the absurd ambitions of the *shaman* and the impossible hopes of the alchemist, the modern chemistry which fulfils them would not be. Always the magician is defeated by 'fate', by the inexorable determinism of things, and it is precisely when he has become conscious of that determinism, and magic has turned into science, that he is able to do in reality the things magic only feigned. Illusion thus plays into the hands of reality. Magic, promising freedom by a blind pressure of the affects, is realised when the emotional content vanishes, when the magician's eyes are opened, and he becomes conscious of the passionless causality of reality.

Magic can only exist, as a confused perception of outer reality, because man is himself confused about his relations with it. He has not distinguished himself from his environment – subjective affects are confused with objective qualities. How does he clear up this confusion? Not by mere contemplation, refusing to handle the pitch lest he become soiled. He separates himself consciously from his environment by struggling with it and actively interpenetrating it, in the course of the development of economic life. When man has grasped the nature of outer reality by his constant struggle with it in economic production, then he understands clearly the distinction between environment and self, because he understands their unity. He learns that man, as a machine, is subject also to necessity, and that the universe, as a process, is the theatre of free development.

How can we separate religion from poetry in the childhood of the race? Both have an economic function and a social content.

We can distinguish them because we find in poetry, in all ages, a characteristic we do not find in religion the more and more clearly it emerges as 'true' religion. Poetry is productive and changeful. The poetry of one age does not satisfy the next age, but each new generation (while appreciating the old poetry) demands poems which more peculiarly and specially express its own problems and aspirations. Thus we have the constant generation of a mass of songs, stories, myths, epics, novels, as a peculiarity of poetic life, which reveals art as something organic and changeful, a flower on the social plant developing and growing with the plant as a whole, because it sucks the same sap, and performs an office that benefits the whole plant.

This incessant change of poetic art is only possible because the appreciator accepts the illusion as illusory. He accepts the phantasy as expressing objective reality while immersed in the phantasy, but, once the phantasy is over, he does not demand that it be still treated as part of the real world. He does not demand a correspondence of all stories and all poetic statements as he demands a correspondence between the experiences of what he calls his real life.

The world may be fairyland in one story, hell in another. Helen may be seized by Paris in one epic, in another she may elude him and die an honoured death in Egypt. Because of this the poet and his hearer are not faced with the problem of integrating the mock worlds of poetry with the real world of everyday existence on the basis of the logical laws of thought – which by no means implies that no integration of any kind takes place. But the poem or novel is accepted as an illusion. We give to the statements of poetic art only a qualified assent, and therefore reality has no vested interest in them. Because of this there is no barrier to the fluent production which is the life of art in all ages.

This too is the characteristic of religion, but only in the early stage, when it is still merged with poetry. Religion is then mythology and shows all the spontaneous inventiveness and recklessness of self-contradiction which is characteristic of mythology.

Why does mythology show this organic characteristic? Because it *is* organic. Because it is still organically connected with society, penetrating every pore. Native races who see an aeroplane presently have a great white bird figuring in their mythology. Early Christianity shows the same insurgent proliferation of mythology so characteristic of art.

A new form of religion begins when the mythologising era ends. The mythology is taken over, but it ossifies. Religion has become 'true' religion.

It is plain that mythology, because of the contradictions it contains, can gain only a special kind of consent from the primitive. It demands from him assent to the illogical. So far Lévy-Bruhl is correct. But this same illogical assent is given by twentieth-century man to the productions of poetry and literary art. Hamlet lives for him. So do the Furies. So does the Inferno. Yet he does not believe in an after-existence in hell or in personal agents of retribution.

True, the assent is not of the same strength with twentieth-century man. The gods live for the primitive in the collective festival and the collective emotion. Because so little division of labour exists, because society is still so undifferentiated, the collective world of emotion in which the gods live penetrates every hour of the individual's life. Not so with the worlds of the theatre or the novel, which segregate themselves from the more complex social life of men. The world of twentieth-century art is more withdrawn – so much so that philosophers continually conceive of it as entirely separate, and advance 'purely' aesthetic criteria – art for art's sake.

But though the strength of the assent differs, the quality is the same. The world of literary art is the world of tribal mythology become sophisticated and complex and self-conscious because man, in his struggle with Nature, has drawn away from her, and laid bare her mechanism and his own by a mutual reflexive action. Mythology with its ritual, and art with its performances, have similar functions – the adaptation of man's emotions to the necessities of social co-operation. Both embody a confused *perception* of society, but an accurate *feeling* of society. Mythology, it is true, has other functions. But we are concerned here with the poetic content of mythology, which afterwards separates itself out as a distinct sphere.

Because mythology so interpenetrates the daily life of the primitive, it demands no overt, formal assent. No Holy Inquisition rams it down people's throats, because in the collective festival it rises vividly from their hearts. Therefore it is flexible. It yields and changes as the tribe's relation to the environment or itself changes. The incursion of an aeroplane or a conqueror produces a corresponding adaptation of the collective mind by a recasting of the always fluid mythology. Hence mythology has a 'self-righting' tendency; it remains on the whole true; it reflects accurately the collective emotional life of the tribe in its relations with the environment to the degree in which the tribe's own interpenetration of its environment in economic production makes accuracy possible.

Why does the age of mythology as a real organic growth give place to the age of dogma and 'true' religion when, because the mythology must now be accepted as true, it ceases to reflect the continual movement of reality and tends to become ossified and dead? Mythology ceases to grow and change and contradict itself, and is set up as something rigid and absolutely true. Faith, a virtue unknown to the primitive, is necessary for its acceptance. Faith was not necessary to the primitive because of his simple direct experience in the world of collective emotion. Faith is not necessary to the novel-reader, because of his immediate direct experience in the world of art. Faith becomes necessary when mythology ossifies into 'true' religion. Faith and dogma are the signs of lack of faith and suspicion of doctrine. They show that mythology has in some way separated itself from society.

How has this come about? Only because society has separated itself from itself; because the matrix of religion has become only a part of society, standing in antagonism to the rest of society. Because of this, religion becomes isolated from the rest of society. 'True' religion marks the emergence of economic classes in society. The end of mythology as a developing thing is the end of undifferentiated tribal life.

Marx has explained how the division of labour demands a class of overseers, village headmen, managers of irrigation works, etc., whose supervision, as differentiation proceeds, gradually passes from administration of the social means of production to that special right or privilege known as ownership of them. The emergence of the ownership of the means of production, as an absolute right, distinct from elective administration of them at society's behest, marks a definite stage in the development of society, the stage of class society. These class divisions rend society in twain, and yet are the only means by which society can pass to higher stages of productive development until a stage is reached generating a class whose economic circumstances enable it to end classes.

The special role of the members of the ruling class as supervisors gives them the means of directing into their own lives all the goods produced by society, save for those needed to ensure the continued existence of the exploited class. Originally chosen as supervisors for 'intellectual' ability, their role, even when it becomes an absolute right and is therefore independent of mental capacity, yet demands primarily mental work, just as the working of the means of production demands primarily manual work. At the same time, the privileged conditions and leisure afforded by consumption of the lion's share of the social product encourages the cultivation of thought and culture among this class, while the hard-driven and beastly condition of the other class discourages this culture.

This rapidly generates a position of increasing instability, like that which causes 'critical' vibration in engineering and in the world of Nature produces in certain species a flare-up of unfavourable adaptations – enormous crests, huge hides, colossal tails and huge protuberances. Like a snowball, the organism increases its own impetus to disaster.

In the same way, once the formation of classes due to division of labour passes a certain stage, the process of cleavage is accelerated. The differentiation of the classes produces on the one hand an exploiting class more and more isolated from reality, more and more concerned with thought, with pleasure, with culture, and on the other hand an exploited class more and more isolated from thought, more and more laborious, more and more subject to circumstances.

This specialisation of function, at first beneficial, eventually becomes pathological. Thought originally separated itself from action, but it only develops by continually returning upon action. It separated from action to guide it. Once from supervisors and leaders, the exploiting class turn to mere enjoyers and parasites, thought has finally separated itself from material reality, and ossifies in a barren formalism or scholasticism. And once from partners and fellow-tribesmen, the exploited class turns to mere slaves, action has finally separated itself from thought and becomes blind mechanism. This is reflected in the life of society as a whole by the decay of culture, science and art in formalism and Alexandrine futility, and the decay of economic production in inefficiency and anarchy. Egypt, China, India, the declining Roman Empire are all examples of this degeneration.

This division of the undifferentiated tribe into a class of supervisors who exercise thought, and a class of workers who only work, is reflected by a similar dichotomy in religion and art. Religion and art cease to be the collective product of the tribe, and become the product of the ruling class who impose a religion just as they impose an act.

A tribe does not give orders to its members to work; their work naturally arises from the collective functioning of the group as a whole, under the pressure of tradition and religion whose genesis we have already examined. Any problem or job can only be solved according to the interests of the tribe as a whole because the tribe is a whole. But when interests are divided, the ruling class orders the ruled. The relation is now coercive.

In the same way, religion becomes dogma. As the class society forms, religion, which continues to function as a confused perception of society, produces a new and more elaborate world of phantasy but one now with a class structure. There is a supreme god in a monarchical society, or family of gods in an autocracy, or a pantheon in a state such as Egypt formed by the syncresis of various developed class units already godded. There are heavenly peers, scribes, priests and captains, corresponding to the division of the earthly ruling class.

Meanwhile the unequal division of goods and the opposed class interests have created an antagonism which divides society. There are outbreaks, rebellions and revolts which must be crushed. Absolute ownership of the means of production, not being thrown up as a natural response to the task confronting the tribe as a whole, is arbitrary, and depends therefore ultimately on violence. It is not made necessary by things and is therefore enforced by men. In the same way, class religion, no longer expressing the collective adaptation of society, must be equally arbitrary. It becomes dogma. A challenge to it is a challenge to the State. Heresy is a civil crime.

The ruling class now seems to dispose of all social labour. With a highly developed agricultural civilisation a god-king is formed at the top of the pyramid, and he seems to wield all social power. The slave by himself seems very small compared with the might of social labour wielded by the god-king. In association the slave wields a tremendous power, the power of building pyramids. But this power does not seem to the slave to be his; it seems to belong to the god-king who directs it. Hence the slave humiliates himself before his own collective power; he deifies the god-king and holds the whole ruling class as sacred. This alienation of self is only a reflection of the alienation of property which has produced it. The slave's humility is the badge not merely of his slavery, but of the power of a society developed to a stage where slavery exists and yields a mighty social power. This power is expressed at the opposite pole to the slave by the divine magnificence of the god-kings of Egypt, China, Japan, and the Sumerian, Babylonian and Accadian city-states. In a syncretic empire like that of Rome, other religions can exist beneath the State cult of the worship of the Emperor. These local cults express local forms of exploitation on which Imperialist exploitation has been imposed, and only a challenge to the god-Emperor is a challenge to Imperial exploitation and therefore a crime in Roman law. As Marx, studying the phenomenon of religion, had perceived as early as 1844:

This State, this society, produces religion – an inverted consciousness of the world – because the world is itself an *inverted world*. Of *this* world Religion is the general theory, its encyclopaedic compendium, its logic in popular form, its spiritual *point d'honneur*, its enthusiasm, its moral sanction, its solemn complement, its general consolation and justification. It is the phantastic realisation of man, because man possesses no true realisation … Religious misery is at once the expression of real misery and a protest against that real misery. [Marx, *On Hegel's Philosophy of Law*]

As society, increasingly rent by this class division, enters on a period of failing economy like that of the declining Roman Empire, the goods produced become less and the share-out more and more coercive. Therefore religion too becomes more and more coercive, more rigid, more tremblingly alive to heresy.

At first the ruling class believes its religion, for differentiation from a primitive mythology has only just taken place. It endeavours therefore to appropriate for itself all the goods of religion, as it is already doing those of society. The best seats in Heaven are taken, or – as with the early rulers of Egypt and the aristocracy of Greece – the Elysian fields are monopolised by them. But as this ruling class is challenged by a restive exploited class, the exploiting class appeases it by sharing with it its own spiritual goods, for these, unlike material goods, do not grow less for being shared. Hence in Egypt immortality was gradually extended even to slaves; and mystery religions, in the decaying Empire, offered to the meanest the deification at first peculiar to the god-Emperor. Thus the increasing misery of the exploited class is reflected in the increasing loveliness of its after-life, provided it leads the good life – i.e. one obedient to its employers. The harvest of phantasy, which in tribal life is always eventually reaped, is for the majority in a class society postponed to a phantastic after-life, because the real harvest also is not consumed by the majority.

This increasing consciousness of the function of religion leads to scepticism on the part of the ruling class itself, which coercively enforces a religion it no longer believes in, and itself takes refuge in an elegant idealism or esoteric philosophy.

Beneath the official religion, which can no more be changed than the system of productive relations which has generated it, lurks a whole undergrowth of 'superstition' and 'legend'. This 'superstition' is simply the mythology of the people, playing its old collective role, but now regarded as something vulgar and ungentlemanly by the ruling class. This superstition itself bears signs that, although collective, its collectiveness is the emasculated homogeneity of an emasculated class. It has a childishness and servility which distinguishes it from the barbarian simplicity of the creations of an undivided society. Sometimes tolerated, sometimes condemned, this superstition shows the adaptive powers of mythology, but it is now an adaptation to the role of an exploited class and is tainted with the idiocy of exploitation. It is full of luck and gold and magic meals and lucky sons – all the fortune this class so conspicuously lacks. But it is genuine, and believed without the need for Faith, precisely because it is not coercively enforced but is the spontaneous production of a collective spirit, and, if not of an undivided society, at least of an undivided class. It is the poetry of religion at a time when religion itself ceases to be poetic. It is the art of the oppressed. Though it fulfils the function of poetry in adapting man's instincts to social life, it cannot be great poetry, for it is no lie that great poetry can only be written by the free. This poetry moves within the boundaries of wish-fulfilment. Its creators have too little spontaneity in their life to be greatly conscious of necessity. It is not therefore ever *tragic* poetry.

Tribal mythology was free and poetic because the undifferentiated economy of the tribe made its members' actions relatively free. This freedom was true freedom – the consciousness of necessity. The job demanded evidently such actions, and they were done spontaneously – by the individual's consciousness of their necessity. Of course this freedom is only relative. It reflects the limited consciousness produced by a limited economy. The divisions of class society were necessary to break the soil for a deeper consciousness and a higher freedom. But still primitive freedom is freedom – such freedom as human society in that stage can know, a stage where, because the economy is undifferentiated, the limited freedom, like the limited product, is at least equally shared by all. Poetry or poetic mythology, fluid and spontaneous, grows in such soil.

In a class society the workers do their tasks blindly as they are told by supervisors. They build pyramids but each contributes a stone; only the rulers know a pyramid is being built. The scale of the undertakings makes possible a greater consciousness of reality, but this consciousness all gathers at the pole of the ruling class. The ruled obey blindly and are unfree.

The rulers are free in the measure of their consciousness. Therefore the exercise of art becomes more and more their exclusive prerogative, reflecting their aspirations and desires. Religion is ossified by the need of maintaining a class right and therefore art now separates itself from religion. Moreover, religion is already disbelieved by the ruling class because of its openly exploitive character. The ossification of religion and the growth of scepticism in a class society is therefore always accompanied by a flourishing of art, the art of the free ruling class, an art which sucks into itself all the fluid, changeful and adaptive characteristics of primitive religion. Religion is now primarily an expression of class coercion, an expression of real misery and a protest against that real misery, while art is now the emotional expression of the ruling class. Sophisticated art of the exploiters sets itself up against the fairy tale and folk art of the exploited. Both flourish for a time side by side.

This stage itself is only transitory. For as the ruling class becomes more and more parasitic, and delegates increasingly its work of supervision, it itself becomes less free. It repeats formally the old consciousness of yesterday, yet the reality it expressed has changed. The class is no longer truly conscious of reality, because it no longer holds the reins, whose pressure on its hands guided it. The exercise of art, like the exercise of supervision, becomes a mechanical repetition by stewards and servants of the forms, functions and operations of the past. Art perishes in a Byzantine formality or an academic conventionality little better than religious dogma. Science becomes mere pedantry – little better than magic. The ruling class has become blind and therefore unfree. Poetry grows in no such soil.

The exploited class too, as this occurs, becomes more exploited and more miserable. The decay of economy, due to the decay of the ruling class, produces a sharper and more bitter exploitation. The cleavage between the rulers and the ruled makes the life of the ruled more mechanical and slavish, and unfree. A peasant or small landholder economy changes to an economy of overlords and serfs. To produce even 'folk' art and 'superstition' a limited spontaneity is necessary. Unlike a class of nomads, smallholders or burghers, a class of slaves has no art. The still essential function of adaptation is now performed for men's minds by a religion whose fixed dogmatism and superstitious faith expresses the lack of spontaneity of the ruled and their diminished consciousness.

Such collapses are not necessarily complete, for between the ruling class and the class which bears the brunt of the exploitation, other classes may develop, in turn to become the ruling class as a result of a revolution. Ossified religions are challenged by heresies which succeed precisely because they express the interests of another class formed secretly by the development of economy and soon to supersede the old. Such heresies are fought as what they are – a challenge to the very existence of the ruling class.

Poetry, then, cannot be separated from the society whose specifically human activity secretes it. Human activity is based on the instinctive. But those forms of human activity which are most changeful and least dependent on instinct are highest and most human. These activities, because they are based on the inheritance from generation to generation of developing forms and systems which are real and material and yet are not environmental in the biological sense, mould in a different way each new generation, which is not however mere clay, for its own inner activity drives on the movement of the external system. This contradiction between individual or natural man, and associated or civilised man, is what makes poetry necessary, and gives it its meaning and its truth. Poetry is a productive or economic activity of man. To separate it from this foundation makes its development impossible to understand.

How far do men's own estimates of the function of poetry at various times agree with our analysis? It has been generally realised by poets such as Milton, Keats, Shelley or Wordsworth that the poet as 'seer', 'prophet' or 'teacher' had a social function of importance. This was not expressed precisely but in a metaphorical way, a poetic way, in which the resounding magnitude of the claims concealed a certain vagueness and poverty of social insight. Indeed the conditions of bourgeois economy – under which poetry tends, like everything else hitherto thought sacred, to become a commodity, and the poet, hitherto thought inspired, tends to become a producer for the anonymous free market – these conditions make it almost impossible for any critic who remains within the categories of bourgeois thought to penetrate the idealistic veils with which poetry in the modern era has concealed her commercialised shame.

Yet it is impossible to appeal to primitive self-appraisement, for literary criticism cannot exist among the unselfconscious primitives – the undifferentiated state of their society makes it unnecessary. The criticism is direct and dumb and efficacious – the valuation of the poet is expressed by the place he is voluntarily accorded in tribal society, the valuation of the poems by their repetition and survival.

In Athens of the fifth century B.C. a society had emerged which, although it was still sufficiently near to primitive society to be conscious of the social function of poetry, was also sufficiently differentiated to be able to separate poetry off as a distinct 'sphere' of culture. Poet as producer is not yet a trade, because Athens is not a capitalistic town engaged chiefly in commodity production. It is a port, a centre of exchange. The vending of poems is therefore a trade – the trade of rhapsodist or paid reciter.

It is a society in ferment, in *revolution*. The developing commerce of the Aegean is producing a class of merchants and slave-owners who are displacing the old land-owning aristocracy. In Athens already the qualifications for rule have ceased to be based on land, and are now based on money income; and this brings it in sharp opposition to Sparta. From a market town and residence of nobles which was a mere appendage of the estates of Attica, Athens has become a town in its own right, a centre of merchants and artisans. This is regarded by the Hellenes as a change from an 'oligarchy' to a 'democracy'. As in later transitions of the same kind, it has taken place through a transitional period of strong, centralised government or 'tyranny' like the Tudor monarchy. The 'democracy' of course is extremely qualified – it is a democracy of men of property. The proletariat has no franchise.

Unlike a somewhat similar stage in medieval economy – the transition from feudalism to capitalism – this is not a class struggle which ends with the clear victory of the revolutionary class, but rather with the 'mutual ruin of the contending classes'. The struggle between the oligarchs and the democrats, between Athens and Sparta, tears Greece to fragments. It is a struggle between town and country, between slave latifundia and slave-town. Because it remains within the categories of slave-owning, it is incapable of a final solution. No decisive stroke is possible such as the freeing of the tied serfs which provides the basis of the bourgeois revolution. Neither class can completely undermine the foundations of the other, for both are based on slavery, and slavery of a similar character.

Culture is still sufficiently undifferentiated for one man to survey the whole, and Plato and Aristotle stand out as philosophers surveying the whole field of culture, including that of literary art. Both were fortunate in that they were born before the class struggle was reaching its final sterile issue in Greece. There had recently been an alliance between the classes against the common enemy, Persia, and the alliance was still dynamic and creative. Plato, spokesman of the oligarchic class, reacts creatively upon Aristotle, who voices the aims and aspirations of the newer class, more tough-minded, more practical, more in touch with reality. It was no accident that Aristotle of Stagira had been so closely allied with Philip and Alexander, for if at last his class were to score a more solid triumph, and to emerge somewhere as conquerors, it was only by bursting the confines of the city and ruling beyond the bounds of Greece in the Hellenistic empires of Alexander's heirs.

Aristotle clearly sees the primitive distinction between private and public speech, between non-rhythmical and rhythmical language, between individual persuasion and collective emotion. Indeed to a Greek of that time, the distinction appeared so self-evident and practical that it needed no explanation. On the one hand was the great instrument of Rhetoric whereby an individual swayed his fellow men; on the other hand the world of Poetics wherein men were collectively moved to emotion. Aristotle writes about both like a man writing a text-book on a useful and important human activity.

Aristotle's view of Rhetoric is simply this – the art of Persuasion. But he makes it clear that he has chiefly in mind the obvious and impressive public occasions where the art of persuasion is needed – in the law courts and the political assemblies. This conception of Rhetoric as individual speech used for formal 'public' occasions must be distinguished from the publicity of poetry. It is the publicity of *State* occasions where State is distinguished from society. Both are one in primitive life, but the class development of Athens has already separated the city from men. The occasions when men use the State machinery and State occasions to persuade others are by Aristotle considered as separate from the occasions when one man speaks to others to persuade them about the normal incidents of daily life. The development of classes has made the city a 'tamer of men', something already towering above society as a structure separate and imposed on it, a view which was to reach its zenith with the Hegelian conception of the absolute State. But it is already implicit in Socrates' refusal to flee the city's judgment of death. In this refusal, Socrates forecasts that the class struggle was doomed to destroy Greece, because the city could not generate a class or even one man able to look beyond the city.

Aristotle's treatment of Poetics requires a more detailed consideration. He deals with a primitive poetry already in process of differentiation in odes, dramas, epics and love poetry, and already distinct from rhetoric; and he therefore looks for a characteristic common to poetic creations which will distinguish them as a species from the non-poetic. An obvious characteristic of poetry to the Greeks was that it told some sort of story. It made some statement about the ways of gods or men or the emotions of the poet which, even though it was not true, seemed true. The epic is a false history, and the drama a feigned action. Even in love poetry the poet may justly say 'I die for love of Chloe' when no Chloe exists. The essence of poetry therefore seemed to the Greeks to be illusion, a conscious illusion.

To Plato this feature of the poet's art appeared so deplorable that he would not admit poets to his Republic, or at least only if their productions were strictly censored. Such reactionary or Fascist philosophies as Plato's are always accompanied by a denial of culture, particularly contemporary culture, and Plato's contemporary culture was pre-eminently poetic. He therefore hates poetry as a philosopher, even though he is charmed by it as a man. In a revolutionary period culture expresses the aspirations of the revolution or the doubts of the dispossessed. The philosophers of the dispossessed regard both the aspirations and the doubts as 'dangerous' or 'corrupt', and want a culture which shores up their rottenness. Such a culture idealises the past in which they were strong. This ideal past does not bear much likeness to the real past, for it is one carefully arranged so that, unlike the real past, it will not again generate the present. For Plato this past is idealised in his *Republic*, ruled by aristocrats and practising a primitive communism which is the way Plato hopes to undermine the trade by which the rival class has come to power.

The Greeks reasoned that poetry was designed to create an illusion. Evidently then the poet made something which created the illusion, even if the something was fabulous. He made stories actually visible on the stage or, as in the Homeric cycle, a history more real than the transactions of the market-place, the reallest thing in the collective life of the Hellenes. This creation the Greeks took to be the special mark of the poet. The very name etymologically was derived from 'making', just as was the Anglo-Saxon word for poet – *makar*.

To build from matter is sublimely great,
But only gods and poets can create.

However, the Greeks did not suppose that a poet could create something out of nothing by words, which are only symbols of reality. They considered that the poet created an artificial imitation of reality, a mimesis. For Plato the poet is essentially a man who mimics the creations of life in order to deceive his hearers with a shadow-world. In this the poet is like the Demiurge, who mocks human dwellers in the cavern of life with shadows of reality.

This theory of mimesis gives Aristotle the specific mark to differentiate between the class of rhetoric and the class of poetry. Though it is, to our modern minds, imperfect as a distinction, owing to the differentiation which has taken place in literature since then, it was an adequate distinction in Aristotle's day.

We separate poetry from the novel and drama; he did not. But the categories of literature are not eternal, any more than the classifications of systematic biology; both must change, as the objects of systematisation evolve and alter in the number and characteristics of their species. Culture changes faster than species, and cultural criticism must be correspondingly flexible. Aristotle's theory of mimesis, as our analysis will show, so far from being superficial, is fundamental for an understanding of the function and method of art.

Aristotle, with his extraverted mind turned firmly on the object, was more interested in the created thing, e.g. the play – than in the man who was influenced by it or who produced it. Thus his angle of attack is aesthetically correct; he does not approach literature like a psychologist or a psycho-analyst.

Plato, with the more intuitive, introverted mind, is interested in the poet and in his hearer rather than the composition itself. His conception of the productive and receptive states of the poetic mind is primitive, corresponding to the more reactionary character of Plato's thought, but behind the barbarity is a cultured snigger which is characteristically Platonic. The barbarity rather than the culture makes Plato to some extent a spokesman of the primitive view of the poet's role, at a time when poetry is passing, as a result of the invention of writing, from a collective to a private phase.

Plato, belonging to the older world of Athens, is not aware of the change. He does not see that the development of Hellenic economy makes the poem an object of exchange between cities and people, like Athenian vases. The poem is no longer, as in old Athenian tragedy, rooted in a collective festival where actors and audience are simultaneously plunged into an associated world of art. Nietzsche's passage from the Dionysian to the Apollonian in art has already taken place as a result of the passage of Athens from the primitive to the sophisticated, i.e. the differentiated. Poems are now separate from the body of society, to be enjoyed by individuals or groups separate from society. And the invention of writing, made necessary by the development of economy to a stage where records and messages were essential because records were no longer the collective memory of the tribe and men no longer lived in common, led to written poems, not simply because writing was invented, but because the needs that demanded writing also demanded that poetry be detached from the collective festival and be enjoyed by men alone. With Euripides even drama becomes a closet art. Plato, however, was only conscious of this in a general way, as expressed in his condemnation of books and the art of writing. Plato's criticisms are like D. H. Lawrence's – they reach back to the past, to the time of an undifferentiated society and collective emotion. They are correct but useless, because the critic is unaware that what he condemns is a product of a class differentiation rooted in economy. He does not therefore reach forward to a solution of present difficulties, but backwards to a time before those difficulties arose. But one cannot put back the clock of history.

Plato is the most charming, humane and civilised of Fascist philosophers, corresponding to a time before the aftermath of the Peloponnesian War had made reaction murderously bitter. In this respect he is an Athenian Hegel. No reactionary philosopher of today could attain Plato's urbanity or charm. This is Plato's conception of the poet:

Socrates is speaking to Ion, a rhapsodist:

It is a divine influence which moves you, like that which resides in the stone called Magnet by Euripides, and Heraclea by the people. For not only does this stone possess the power of attracting iron rings, but it can communicate to them the power of attracting other rings; so that you may see sometimes a long chain of rings and other iron substances, attached and suspended one to the other by this influence. And as the power of the stone circulates through all the links of the series, and attaches each to each, so the Muse, communicating through those whom she has first inspired, to all others capable of that first enthusiasm, creates a chain and a succession. For the authors of those great poems which we admire, do not attain to excellence through the rules of any art, but they utter their beautiful melodies of verse in a state of inspiration, and, as it were, possessed by a spirit not their own. Thus the composers of lyrical poetry create those admired songs of theirs in a state of divine insanity, like the Corybantes, who lose all control of their reason in the enthusiasm of the sacred dance; and, during this supernatural possession, are excited to the rhythm and harmony which they communicate to men. Like the Bacchantes who, when possessed by the god, draw honey and milk from the rivers, in which, when they come to their senses, they find nothing but simple water. For the souls of the poets, as poets tell us, have this peculiar ministration in the world. They tell us that these souls, flying like bees from flower to flower, and wandering over the gardens and the meadows and the honey-flowing fountains of the Muses, return to us laden with the sweetness of melody; and, arrayed as they are in the plumes of rapid imagination, they speak truth. For a poet is indeed a thing ethereally light, winged and sacred, nor can he compose anything worth calling poetry until he becomes inspired, and, as it were, mad, or whilst any reason remains in him. For whilst a man retains any portion of the thing called reason, he is utterly incompetent to produce poetry or to vaticinate. Every rhapsodist or poet, whether dithyrambic, encomiastic, choral, epic, or iambic, is excellent in proportion to the extent of his participation in the divine influence, and the degree in which the Muse itself has descended upon him. In other respects, poets may be sufficiently ignorant and incapable. For they do not compose according to any art which they have acquired, but from the impulse of the divinity within them; for did they know any rules of criticism according to which they could compose beautiful verses upon any one subject, they would be able to exert the same faculty in respect to all or any other. The god seems purposely to have deprived all poets, prophets, and soothsayers of every particle of reason and understanding, the better to adapt them to their employment as his ministers and interpreters; and that we, their auditors, may acknowledge that those who write so beautifully, are possessed, and address us inspired by the god. [*Ion*, translated by Shelley]

Here Plato shows poetry to be something different in kind from conscious rhetoric, the art of persuasion, which, according to Greek views, could be reduced to rule and learned. But poetry can never be learned, for according to Plato it is not a conscious function, with rules of criticism, but an inpouring of the god, and he is sufficiently near to primitive culture to place the poet beside the prophet and the soothsayer. Moreover, according to Plato's view, this inspiration is not only essential for the poet, but for his reader. The rhapsodist who declaims him, and the auditor who is affected by him, must also be inspired by the god. In other words, not only the writing but also the appreciation of poetry is an unconscious (or irrational) function. To Plato all deception is a form of enchantment. Poets are wizards wielding quasi-religious powers. Plato's symbol of the magnetised rings well expresses the collective character of primitive poetry. In contrast to Aristotle, Plato the idealist is concerned with the enjoyment rather than the function of poetry.

Aristotle, however, is uninterested in the poet's mind, and does not concern himself with whether or not the creation and appreciation of poetry is a conscious function. He judges it by results, by poems. He systematises them, analyses them, and reduces them to rule. He finds that mimesis is the distinguishing feature of Poetics, and he investigates the rules for producing a convincing and successful mimesis.

Unlike Plato, he goes further. As befits a philosopher who studied the constitutions of existing states, he asks: what is the social function of tragedy?

His answer is well known. Its effect is *cathartic* – purging. The answer is somewhat enigmatic, once one attempts to go behind it. It is tempting to give to the expression a modern interpretation. It has been suggested, for example, that this is merely the basic therapy of Freudism – therapy by abreaction – in a Greek dress. This is on the one hand an over-refinement of Aristotle, and on the other hand a misunderstanding of what therapy by abreaction actually is. Poetic creations, like other phantasies, may be the vehicle of neurotic conflicts or complexes. But a phantasy is the cloak whereby the 'censor' hides the unconscious complex. So far from this process being cathartic, it is the opposite according to Freud's own principles. To cure the basic complex by abreaction the phantasy must be stripped of its disguise and the infantile and archaic kernel laid bare.

Thus the poetic construct, according to Freud's own empirical discoveries, cannot represent an abreactive therapy even for the poet. But Aristotle visualises tragedy as cathartic for the *spectators*. Even if the poetic phantasy did have an abreactive effect on the poet, it is impossible that every spectator should have not only the same complex as the poet, but the same associations, which analysis shows are generally highly personal.

Hence followers of Freud who suggest that Aristotle's *catharsis* is the equivalent of Freud's *therapy by abreaction*, not only misunderstand

Aristotle, but also are imperfectly acquainted with the empirical discoveries on which psycho-analysis rests.

It is best, in fact, not to go behind Aristotle's simple conception, until we ourselves are clear as to the function of poetry, and can compare Aristotle's ideas with our own. How Aristotle arrived at his definition is fairly clear. On the one hand he saw tragedy arousing unpleasant emotions in the spectator – fear and anxiety and grief. On the other hand these same spectators went away feeling the better for it, so much so that they returned for more. The emotions, though unpleasant, had done them good. In the same way unpleasant medicaments do people good, and perhaps Aristotle went further, and visualised the tragedy concentrating and driving out of the mind the unpleasant emotions, just as a purge concentrates and drives out of the body the unpleasant humours. This highly practical attitude towards tragedy is not only, as it seems to me, healthy, and good literary criticism, but essentially Greek. If the tragedy did not make the Athenians feel better, in spite of its tragedy, it was bad. The tragic poet who made them weep bitterly at the fate of their fellow Hellenes in Persia was fined. A similar imposition suggests itself for our own purely sentimental war literature.

This, then, was the intelligent Greek view of literature as the differentiation, carried so far in our own culture, had just begun. On the one hand Rhetoric, the art of persuasion, exercised consciously and appreciated consciously, an art which was simply ordinary conversation hypostatised by the hypostasis of the city-state. On the other hand Poetics, a mimesis whose success in imitating reality can be judged by the poignancy of the emotions roused, just as if the auditors were really concerned in it. Both Plato and Aristotle agree here. But in Plato's view no rules can be laid down for achieving that poignancy, for both creation and appreciation come from outside the conscious mind. Plato, moreover, sees no social justification for poetry. 'The emotions aroused,' retorts Aristotle, 'serve a social end, that of *catharsis*.'

Such a definition of poetry is insufficient in literature today, not because the Greeks were wrong but because literature, like society, has changed. If he were systematising literature today, Aristotle would see that the criterion of mimesis was insufficient to distinguish the existing species of literature, not because of any weakness in the original definition, but simply because in the course of social evolution new forms of literature had arisen. Mimesis is characteristic also of the modern novel and prose play. What we nowadays agree to call poetry is something apart from both play and novel, for which fresh specific differences must be sought. Our next task is to find them.

But Aristotle's definition reminds us that we cannot, in studying the sources of poetry, ignore the study of other forms of literature, because there is a time when all literature is poetry. A materialistic approach to culture avoids any such error. We have already seen that there is a time when all religion as well as all literature is poetry. Yet as moderns, as men living in the age of capitalism, our concern must be principally with bourgeois poetry. Our next section therefore will be devoted to a general historical study of the development of modern poetry.

6

The Development of Modern Poetry

* * *

The fact that England for three centuries led the world in the development of capitalism and that, during the same period, it led the world in the development of poetry, are not unrelated coincidences but part of the same movement of history.

The bourgeoisie, historically, has played a most revolutionary part.

The bourgeoisie, wherever it has got the upper hand, has put an end to all feudal, patriarchal, idyllic relations. It has pitilessly torn asunder the motley feudal ties that bound man to his 'natural superiors', and has left no other nexus between man and man than naked self-interest, than callous 'cash payment'.

The bourgeoisie cannot exist without constantly revolutionising the means of production, and thereby the relations of production, and with them the whole relations of society. Conservation of the old modes of production in unaltered form was, on the contrary, the first condition of existence for all earlier industrial classes. Constant revolutionising of production, uninterrupted disturbance of all social conditions, everlasting uncertainty and agitation distinguish the bourgeois epoch from all earlier ones. All fixed fast-frozen relations, with their train of ancient and venerable prejudices and opinions, are swept away, all new-formed ones become antiquated before they can ossify. All that is solid melts into air, all that is holy is profaned, and man is at last compelled to face with sober senses his real conditions of life and his relations with his kind. [Marx and Engels, *The Communist Manifesto*, 1848]

Capitalist poetry reflects these conditions. It is the outcome of these conditions. The birth of poetry took place from the undifferentiated matrix of the tribe, which gave it a mythological character. It separated itself from religion as the art of a ruling class in class society, but, except in moments of revolutionary transition like that of fourth century B.C. Greece, this art led a quiet existence, mirroring the slow rise and slow collapse of a class 'whose first condition of existence is conservation of its mode of production in unaltered form'. Then a class developed beneath the quiet, stiff art of feudalism, whose vigour is first announced by the Gothic cathedrals. This class in turn became a ruling class, but one whose condition of existence is a constant revolution of the means of production, and thereby the relations of production, and with them the whole relations of society.

Its art is therefore in its essence an insurgent, non-formal, naturalistic art. Only the art of revolutionary Greece in any way forecasts the naturalism of bourgeois art. It is an art which constantly revolutionises its own conventions, just as bourgeois economy constantly revolutionises its own means of production. This constant revolution, this constant sweeping-away of 'ancient and venerable prejudices and opinions', this 'everlasting uncertainty and agitation', distinguishes bourgeois art from all previous art. Any bourgeois artist who even for a generation rests upon the conventions of his time becomes 'academic' and his art lifeless. This same movement is characteristic of English poetry.

The characteristic of capitalist economy is that it apparently sweeps away all directly coercive relations between men – and seems to substitute for them the coercive relations of men to a thing – the State-upheld right to property. Men are no longer coercively tied together, as in a feudal society serf is tied to lord and lord to overlord, but they produce independently for the free market, and buy independently from this same free market. They take not merely their products but their abilities to the market and are entitled to sell their labour-power there without let or hindrance to the highest bidder. This unreserved access to an unrestricted market constitutes the 'freedom' of capitalist society.

Thus there appear to be no coercive relations between men, but only force-upheld relations between men and a thing (property) which result in relations between an individual and the market. The market seems to be a part of Nature, a piece of the environment, subject to natural 'laws' of supply and demand. Its coercion does not seem the coercion of men, but of blind natural forces, like a gale or volcanic eruption.

In fact the market is nothing but the blind expression of real relations between men. These relations are relations of coercion, the characteristic exploitation of capitalism by ownership of the means of production and the purchase of the labour-power of the free labourer – free of all property but his bare hands. But just because it is a blind expression, it is coercive and anarchic, and acts with the violence and uncontrolled recklessness of a natural force. Just because the coercive relations between capitalist and wage-labourer are veiled, they are so much the more brutal and shameless.

Capitalist economy, therefore, is the economy of a sham individualism and a hollow freedom for the majority. The condition of existence of the bourgeois class as a ruling class, and therefore the condition of its freedom in society, is the absence of directly coercive relations between man and man. Such coercive relations are restrictions – like the feudal restrictions which bind serf to lord. But freedom without social relations would be no freedom at all, but only a blind anarchy in which society must perish. In addition, therefore, to the absence of direct relations between men, bourgeois society must include the presence of rights to absolute ownership of means of production – the right of 'private property'. This absolute right is maintained by the device of a coercive State power, with its laws and police and army, which, because it enforces a property right and not any direct ownership of men by men, seems to tower over society as something mediating and independent. But in fact, since this property right gives the bourgeois coercive power over the 'free' labourer through ownership of the means of production, both the State and the bourgeois economy it enforces veil a coercive society for the majority, and the only freedom it contains is the freedom of the bourgeois from nature – due to his monopolisation of the social product – and his freedom from human coercion – due to the elimination from society of all directly coercive relations of a feudal character. Seen from the viewpoint of the bourgeois, bourgeois society is a free society whose freedom is due to its individualism, to its completely free market and its absence of direct social relations, of which absence the free market is the cause and expression. But to the rest of society bourgeois society is a coercive society whose individualism and free market is the method of coercion. This is the basic contradiction of bourgeois society, which must be grasped to understand the whole movement which secures the development of capitalist culture.

We saw in our analysis of the birth of poetry that early poetry is essentially collective emotion, and is born in the group festival. It is not collective emotion of an unconditioned, instinctive kind, such as might be roused in a herd by a foe; it is the collective emotion of a response conditioned by the needs of economic association.

Now bourgeois culture is the culture of a class to whom freedom – man's realisation of all his instinctive powers – is secured by 'individualism'. It might therefore seem that bourgeois civilisation should be anti-poetic, because poetry is collective and the bourgeois is an individualist.

But this is to take the bourgeois *at his own valuation*. Certainly we must first of all do this, whether to understand him as capitalist or as poet. The bourgeois sees himself as an heroic figure fighting a lone fight for freedom – as the individualist battling against all the social relations which fetter the natural man, who is born free and is for some strange reason everywhere in chains. And in fact his individualism does lead to a continual technical advance and therefore to an increasing freedom. His fight against feudal social relations permits a great release of the productive forces of society. His individualism expresses the particular way in which the bourgeois economy continually revolutionises the base on which it stands, until the base becomes too much for the superstructure, and bourgeois economy explodes into its opposite.

And, in the same way, the bourgeois poet sees himself as an individualist striving to realise what is most *essentially* himself by an expansive outward movement of the energy of his heart, by a release of internal forces which outward forms are crippling. This is the bourgeois dream, the dream of the one man alone producing the phenomena of the world. He is Faust, Hamlet, Robinson Crusoe, Satan and Prufrock.

This 'individualism' of the bourgeois, which is born of the need to dissolve the restrictions of feudal society, causes a tremendous and ceaseless technical advance in production. In the same way it causes in poetry a tremendous and ceaseless advance in technique.

But both capitalist and poet become darker figures – first tragic, then pitiful and finally vicious. The capitalist finds his very individualism, his very freedom, producing all the blind coercion of war, anarchy, slump and revolution. The machine in its productiveness finally threatens even him. The market in its blindness becomes a terrifying force of nature.

By means of the market, capitalist constantly hurls down fellow capitalist into wage-labour or relegates him to the ranks of the temporarily privileged 'salariat'. The artisan of yesterday is the factory hand of today. The shop-owner of this year is the chain-store manager of the next year. Last week, owner of a small business – today, salaried executive in a large trust: this is the dramatic process whereby capitalism revolutionises itself. It does so by means of the very free market on which the bourgeois depends for freedom. This guarantee of individualism and independence produces the very opposite – trustification and dependence on finance capital. This golden garden of fair competition produces the very opposite of fairness: price-cutting, wars, cartels, monopolies, 'corners' and vertical trusts. But all these evils seem to the bourgeois, who is hurled from his freedom by them, to be – as indeed they are – direct and coercive social relations and he revolts against them as the very opposite of his ideal recipe, the free market. He therefore revolts against them by demanding a fairer market and keener competition, without realising that since these ills are created by the free market, to demand the intensification of its freedom is to demand an intensification of the slavery he hates. He therefore drives on the movement he detests, and can only escape by escaping from the bourgeois contradiction. The bourgeois is always talking about liberty because it is always slipping from his grasp.

The bourgeois poet treads a similar circle. He finds the loneliness which is the condition of his freedom unendurable and coercive. He finds more and more of his experience of the earth and the universe unfriendly and a restraint on his freedom. He ejects everything social from his soul, and finds that it deflates, leaving him petty, empty and insecure.

How has this come about? We can only discover why if we now cease to take the bourgeois at his own valuation, and lay bare the economic motion of which his own valuation of himself is the reflection. At each stage the bourgeois finds that his abolition of social 'restrictions' leads to their intensification. His drive towards a free market exposes the producer to a gale of competition of which the only outcome is – an amalgamation. His destruction of feudal 'complexities' in favour of the simple bourgeois right to property produces all the staggering elaboration of the bourgeois law of contract. His hate of feudal rule and social coercion produces the strongly centralised, bourgeois State with its endless petty interferences with the liberty of the individual. Individualism has produced anti-individualism. The very economy whose mission it seemed to be to sweep away all social relations, produces a society more overwhelmingly complex than any hitherto known. His demand for freedom is a negation of freedom. He is a 'mirror revolutionary' and continually revolutionises society by asking for that which will procure the opposite of what he desires.

This self-contradictory movement is given in the fundamental law of capitalist production. It is a result of the same law which brings about a price-cutting war, in which each capitalist is compelled to ruin the other, and cannot do otherwise, for to delay the final ruin of all would ensure his earlier extinction. This movement produces the continual increase of constant capital in every industry, which leads to a falling rate of interest and causes the familiar capitalist crisis, from which recovery is only possible by means of the destruction of a large portion of the country's wealth. This same contradiction produces also the expansive growth of capitalism, its constant revolution of its own basis and its eager pressure into every corner of the world. It produces a continual amalgamation and trustification which, by increasing the proportion of constant capital, only accelerates the falling rate of profit.

This contradiction in capitalist production, which secures its revolutionary expansion, also brings about its revolutionary decline. When the expansive powers of capitalism have laid the whole world under tribute, the rival centres of advance clash against each other in concealed or open war, only to intensify in each other the causes which demand expansion. The productive forces strain at the productive relations. There is a final crisis of 'over-production'. The falling rate of profit, unavoidable fruit of the self-contradiction in the heart of capitalism, becomes apparent in mass unemployment, a world crisis, a general slowing-down of capitalist expansion, war and revolution. And this final movement, in which the bourgeois finds his charter of freedom the very bond that seals him slave to necessity, is reflected also in his poetry, in the poetry of Imperialism and Fascism.

The very destruction of all direct social coercion – which was the condition of bourgeois pre-eminence and therefore freedom – is the condition of slavery for the exploited and expropriated, because it is the means of maintaining the indirect coercion of capital, and for this uses the openly coercive machinery of the State. Therefore in the latter part of capitalist development, the bourgeois finds himself confronted by a class, the means of whose freedom is an organisation into trade unions, which alleviate the rigour of the free market. These can only secure freedom for themselves by imposing coercive restrictions on him. This class is the class of wage-labourers or proletarians. Organising themselves first as Chartists, then in the trade unions, and finally led by a conscious political party, they impose on the capitalist coercive restrictions, such as the Factory Acts, social insurance and the like, which are the conditions of such liberty as they can obtain within the categories of bourgeois economy. But each class's freedom secures the unfreedom of the other – that is the contradiction which now comes nakedly to light.

Bourgeois production imposes on this class the means of organisation. Bourgeois economy groups its members in towns and factories and makes them work in co-operation. The bourgeois class temporarily buried the competition of men and appealed to the brotherhood of men whenever it required their alliance to overthrow feudal restrictions; and this gave the wage-labourers a political education and led to the formation of their political party.

This new class finally secures its own freedom by a complete executive organisation of itself as a *ruling* class – the Soviets of workers' power – and imposes on the bourgeoisie the final 'freedom' of release from ownership of private property, thus exposing the lie on which the bourgeois notion of freedom was based. But with the disappearance of the bourgeoisie the last coercive relation rooted in the necessities of economic production disappears, and man can set about becoming genuinely free.

This proletarian revolution is accomplished in circumstances which necessarily uproot and proletarianise numbers of the bourgeoisie themselves:

> Just as therefore, at an earlier period, a section of the nobility went over to the bourgeoisie, so now a portion of the bourgeoisie goes over to the proletariat, and in particular a portion of the bourgeois ideologists who have raised themselves to the level of comprehending theoretically the historical movement as a whole. They thus defend not their present, but their future interests; they desert their own standpoint to place themselves at that of the proletariat. [*The Communist Manifesto*]

This desertion of the bourgeois ideologists to defend their future interests, in the final movement of capitalism, is also reflected in English poetry.

We cannot therefore understand the fundamental movement of capitalist poetry unless we understand that the self-contradiction which drives on the development of bourgeois poetry so rapidly and restlessly is the ideological counterpart of the self-contradiction which produces the increasing movement of capitalist economy and is the cause of the growth of constant capital, the falling rate of profit, and the recurrent capitalist crisis. What the bourgeois encounters in real life necessarily moulds his ideal experience. The collective world of art is fed by the collective world of real society because it is built of materials which derive their structure and emotional associations from social use.

To the bourgeois, freedom is not the consciousness of necessity but the ignorance of it. He stands society on its head. To him the instincts are 'free', and society everywhere puts them in chains. This is the reflection, not only of his revolt against feudal restrictions, but of capitalism's continual revolt against its own conditions, which at every step drives it forward to revolutionise its own base.

The bourgeois is a man who believes in an inborn spontaneity which secures man's free will. He does not see that man is only free in so far as he is conscious of the motive of his actions – as opposed to involuntary actions of a reflex character, like a tic, or imposed actions of a coercive character, like a shove in the back. To be conscious of the motive is to be conscious of the cause, that is of the necessity. But the bourgeois protests against this, because determinism seems to him the antithesis of free will.

To be conscious of one's motives is to will freely – to be conscious of the necessity of one's actions. Not to be conscious is to act instinctively like an animal, or blindly like a man propelled by a push from behind his back. This consciousness is not secured by introspection but by a struggle with reality which lays bare its laws, and secures to man the means of consciously using them.

The bourgeois refusal to acknowledge this is paralleled by his attitude to society, in which he thinks he is free if he is free from overt social duties – the restrictions of feudalism. But at the same time the conditions of capitalist production demand that he enter into an increasingly complex series of relations with his fellow men. These, however, appear as relations to an objective market controlled by the laws of supply and demand. He is therefore unconscious of their true nature and ignorant of the real determinism of society that has him in its grasp. Because of this he is unfree. He is ruined by blind forces; he is subject to crises, wars, and slumps and 'unfair' competition. His actions produce these things, although he is undesirous of producing them.

In so far as man understands the laws of outer reality – the determinism or necessity of dead nature as expressed by science – he is free of nature, as is shown by machines. Freedom here too is the consciousness of necessity. The bourgeois is able to attain to this freedom, which is lacking in earlier class societies. But this freedom is dependent not on the individual but on associated men. The more elaborate the machine, the more elaborate the association needed to operate it. Hence man cannot be really free of nature without being conscious of the laws of association in society. And the more the possibility of being really free develops with the development of machinery, the more rudely he is reminded of the slavery of ignorance.

In so far as man understands the nature of society – the determinism which connects the consciousness and productive relations of men – he can control society's impact upon himself as an individual and on nature as a social force. But the very conditions of bourgeois economy demand that social relations be veiled by the free market and by the forms of commodity production, so that relations between men are disguised as relations to things. The bourgeois regards any demand that man should control economic production and become conscious of determinism as 'interference with liberty'. And it is an interference with liberty in this respect, that it interferes with his status as a bourgeois and his privileged position in society – the privilege of monopolising the products and therefore the freedom of society.

Thus the root of the bourgeois illusion regarding freedom and the function of society in relation to the instincts, is seen to spring from the essential contradiction of bourgeois economy – private (i.e. individual) property in social means of production. The bourgeois ceases to be bourgeois as soon as he becomes conscious of the determinism of his social relations, for consciousness is not mere contemplation, it is the product of an active process. It is generated by his experiments in controlling social relations, just as his consciousness of Nature's determinism is generated by his experiments in controlling her. But before men can control their social relations, they must have the power to do so – that is, the power to control the means of production on which social relations rest. But how can they do this when these means are in the power of a privileged class?

The condition of freedom for the bourgeois class in a feudal society is the non-existence of feudal rule. The condition of the freedom of the workers in a capitalist society is the non-existence of capitalist rule. This is also the condition of freedom for a completely free society – that is, a classless society. Only in such a society can all men actively develop their consciousness of social determinism by controlling their associated destinies. The bourgeois can never accept this definition of freedom for all until he has ceased to be a bourgeois and comprehended the historical movement as a whole.

The nature of this contradiction in the bourgeois notion of freedom only becomes apparent in so far as bourgeois society decays, and the freedom of the bourgeois class becomes increasingly antagonistic to the freedom of society as a whole. The freedom of society as a whole consists in its economic products. These represent the freedom man has won in his struggle with Nature. In proportion as these expand, not only does the bourgeois feel himself free, thanks to the conditions of bourgeois economy, but the rest of society, which shares these products, is not proposed to challenge these conditions in a revolutionary way. It also – passively – accepts them. All this seems therefore a confirmation of the bourgeois theory of freedom. In these particular circumstances the bourgeois theory of freedom is true. It is an illusion, a phantastic illusion, which at this stage *realises* itself in practice. Man *is* gaining freedom by denying the relations of society, for these were feudal relations, already made obsolete by the development of bourgeois economy in their pores.

> But in order to oppress a class, certain conditions must be assured to it under which it can, at least, continue its slavish existence. The serf, in the period of serfdom, raised himself to membership in the commune, just as the petty bourgeois, under the yoke of feudal absolutism, managed to develop into a bourgeois. The modern labourer, on the contrary, instead of rising with the progress of industry, sinks deeper and deeper below the conditions of existence of his own class. He becomes a pauper, and pauperism develops more rapidly than population and wealth. And here it becomes evident that the bourgeoisie is unfit any longer to be the ruling class in society and to impose its conditions of existence upon society as an overriding law. It is unfit to rule because it is incompetent to assure an existence to its slave within his slavery, because it cannot help letting him sink into such a state, that it has to feed him instead of being fed by him. Society can no longer live under this bourgeoisie: in other words, its existence is no longer compatible with society. [*The Communist Manifesto*]

At this point, therefore, the contradictory nature of the bourgeois definition of freedom discloses itself because the advance of society has objectively negated it. This, therefore, gives way to a definition of freedom as a consciousness of determinism, and the condition of man's freedom is now seen to be the consciousness and the control of the determining causes of social relations – the productive forces. But this is a revolutionary demand – a demand for socialism and proletarian power, and it is opposed by the bourgeois as the negation of freedom – as indeed it is for him, as a bourgeois. He attempts to speak here in the name of all society, but the revolutionary movement of the bulk of society itself denies him this right.

Thus the bourgeois illusion regarding freedom, which counterposes freedom and individualism to determinism and society, overlooks the fact that society is the instrument whereby man, the unfree individual, in association realises his freedom and that the conditions of such association are the conditions of freedom. This illusion is itself the product of a particular class society, and a reflection of the special privilege on which bourgeois rule rests, and which rends society in two as long as it persists.

Other class societies have their own illusions. Thus a slave-owning society sees freedom, not in the absence of coercive relations, but in a special coercive relation, that of Will, in which the lord directs, and the slave blindly obeys as of right. In such a society, to be free is to will. But the development of classes sunders the consciousness that directs the will from the reality with which the slave, who blindly obeys the will, must actively struggle. The economic decline which results from this is a reflection of unfreedom due to man's increasing unconsciousness of necessity, due to the increasing inactivity of the class which is supposed to be the vehicle of consciousness and therefore of freedom. Consciousness is generated by man's active struggle with Nature, and perishes in a blind formalism once that grapple ceases.

To be aware of the true nature of freedom – that it involves consciousness of the determinism of the environment and of man and of the society which expresses their mutual struggle – to be aware of this, not as a result of contemplation, which cannot generate consciousness, but in active struggle, is to be engaged in a struggle to end those very relations of blind coercion or exploitation in society which obstruct the development of this consciousness. To end them is to end classes and give men the means of becoming truly free: but this can only happen because capitalism has evolved its own grave-digger – the class whose conditions of existence not only drive it to revolt and make possible a successful rule, but also ensure that its rule can only be based on an extinction of all rights which can produce classes.

* * *

All bourgeois poetry is an expression of the movement of the bourgeois illusion, according as the contradiction rooted in bourgeois economy emerges in the course of the development of capitalism. Men are not blindly moulded by economy; economy is the result of their actions, and its movement reflects the nature of men. Poetry is then an expression of the real essence of associated men and derives its truth from this.

The bourgeois illusion is then seen to be a phantasy and bears the same relation to truth as the phantasy of primitive mythology. In the collective festival, where poetry is born, the phantastic world of poetry anticipates the harvest and, by so doing, makes possible the real harvest. But the illusion of this collective phantasy is not a mere drab copy of the harvest yet to be: it is a reflection of the emotional complex involved in the fact that man must stand in a certain relation to others and to the harvest, that his instincts must be adapted in a certain way to Nature and other men, to make the harvest possible. The collective poetry of the festival, although it is a confused perception of the real harvest-to-be, is an accurate picture of the instinctive adaptations involved in associated man's relation to the harvest process. It is a real picture of man's heart.

In the same way bourgeois poetry reflects, in all its variety and complexity, the instinctive adaptations of men to each other and Nature necessary in those social relations which will produce freedom – for freedom, as we saw, is merely man's phantastic and poetic expression for the economic product of society which secures his self-realisation. We include of course in this economic product not merely the commercial or saleable product of society, but the cultural and emotional products, including men's consciousnesses themselves. Hence this bourgeois illusion regarding freedom, of which bourgeois poetry is the expression, has a reality in so far as it produces, by its existence, freedom – I do not mean in any formal sense, I mean that just as primitive poetry is justified by the material harvest it produces, which is the means of the primitive's freedom, so bourgeois poetry is justified by the material product of the society which generates it in its movement. But it is a freedom not of all society, but of the bourgeois class which appropriates the major part of society's products.

For freedom is not a state, it is a specific struggle with Nature. Freedom is always relative, relative to the success of the struggle. The consciousness of the nature of freedom is not the simple contemplation of a metaphysical problem, but the very act of living and behaving like a man in a certain state of society. Each stage of consciousness is definitely won; it is only maintained as a living thing by social movement – the movement we call labour. The working-out of the bourgeois illusion concerning freedom, first as a triumphant truth (the growth and increasing prosperity of capitalism), next as a gradually revealed lie (the decline and final crisis of capitalism) and finally as its passage into its opposite, freedom as the life-won consciousness of social necessity (the proletarian revolution), is a colossal movement of men, materials, emotions and ideas, it is a whole history of toiling, learning, suffering and hoping men. Because of the scale, energy and material complexity of the movement, bourgeois poetry is the glittering, subtle, complex, many-sided thing it is. The bourgeois illusion which is also the condition of freedom for the bourgeoisie is realised in their own poetry, because bourgeois poets, like the rest of the bourgeoisie, realise it in their lives, in all its triumphant emotion, its tragedy, its power of analysis and its spiritual disgust. And the consciousness of social necessity which is the condition of freedom for the people as a whole in classless, communist society, will be realised in communist poetry because it can only be realised in its essence, not as a metaphysical formula, but by living as men in a developing communist society, which includes living as poets and readers of poetry.

The bourgeois sees man's instincts – his 'heart', source of his desires and aims – as the source of his freedom. This is false inasmuch as the instincts *unadapted* are blind and unfree. But when adapted by the relations of society they give rise to emotions, and these adaptations, of which the emotions are the expression and mirror, are the means whereby the instinctive energy of man is diverted to drive the machine of society: the machine of society, revolving, enables man to face Nature and struggle with her, not as individual, instinctive man but as associated, adapted men. Thus the instincts drive on the movement which secures man's freedom. This illusion and this truth about the relation of the instincts to freedom and society work themselves out in bourgeois poetry and constitute its secret energy and constant life. Thus, knowing the essence of this bourgeois illusion to be a special belief concerning 'individualism' or the 'natural man', which in turn derives from the conditions of bourgeois economy, we cannot be surprised that the bourgeois poet is the lonely man who, apparently turning away from society into himself, by so doing expresses the more strongly the essential relations of contemporary society. Bourgeois poetry is individualistic because it expresses the collective emotion of its era.

* * *

7
English Poets I:
The Period of Primitive Accumulation

Capitalism requires two conditions for its existence – masses of capital and 'free' – i.e. expropriated – wage-labourers. Once the movement has started, capitalism generates its own conditions for further development. The sum of constant capital grows by accumulation and aggregates by amalgamation, and this amalgamation, by continually expropriating artisans and other petty bourgeoisie, produces the necessary supply of wage-labourers.

A period of primitive accumulation is therefore necessary before these conditions can be realised. This primitive accumulation must necessarily be violent and forcible, for the bourgeoisie, not yet a ruling class, has not yet created the political conditions for its own expansion: the State is not yet a bourgeois state.

In England during this period the bourgeoisie and that section of the nobility which had gone over to the bourgeoisie, seized the Church lands and treasure and created a horde of dispossessed vagrants by the enclosure of common lands, the closing of the monasteries, the extension of sheep-farming, and the final extinction of the feudal lords with their retainers. The seizure of gold and silver from the New World also played an important part in providing a base for capitalism. This movement was possible because the monarchy, in its fight with the feudal nobility, leant on the bourgeois class and in turn rewarded them for their support. The Tudor monarchs were autocrats in alliance with the bourgeoisie and bourgeoisified nobility.

In this period of primitive accumulation the conditions for the growth of the bourgeois class are created lawlessly. To every bourgeois it seems as if his instincts – his 'freedom' – are intolerably restricted by laws, rights and restraints, and that beauty and life can only be obtained by the violent expansion of his desires.

* * *

Elizabethan poetry tells a story. The story always deals with men's individualities as realised in economic functions – it sees them from the outside as 'characters' or 'types'. It sites them in a real social world seen from the outside. But in the era of primitive accumulation, bourgeois economy has not differentiated to an extent where social 'types' or 'norms' have been stabilised. Bourgeois man believes himself to be establishing an economic role by simply realising his character, like a splay foot. The instinctive and the economic seem to him naturally one: it is only the feudal roles which seem to him forced and 'artificial'. Hence the story and poetry are not yet antagonistic: they have not yet separated out.

In this era of primitive accumulation all is fluid and homogeneous. Bourgeois society has not created its elaborate division of labour, to which the elaborate complexity of culture corresponds. Today psychology, biology, logic, philosophy, law, poetry, history, economics, novel-writing, the essay, are all separate spheres of thought, each requiring specialisation for their exploration and each using a specialised vocabulary. But men like Bacon and Galileo and da Vinci did not specialise, and their language reflects this lack of differentiation. Elizabethan tragedy speaks a language of great range and compass, from the colloquial to the sublime, from the technical to the narrative, because language itself is as yet undifferentiated.

Like all great language, this has been bought and paid for. Tyndale paid for it with his life; the English prose style as a simple and clear reality, fit for poetry, was written in the fear of death, by heretics for whom it was a religious but also a revolutionary activity demanding a bareness and simplicity which scorned all trifling ornament and convention. Nothing was asked of it but the truth.

These facts combined make it possible for Elizabethan poetry to be drama and story, collective and undifferentiated, and yet express with extraordinary power the vigour of the bourgeois illusion in the era of primitive accumulation.

Shakespeare could not have achieved the stature he did if he had not exposed, at the dawn of bourgeois development, the whole movement of the capitalist contradiction, from its tremendous achievement to its mean decline. His position, his feudal 'perspective', enabled him to comprehend in one era all the trends which in later eras were to separate out and so be beyond the compass of one treatment. [In the same way More, from his feudal perspective, anticipates the development of capitalism into communism in his *Utopia*.] It was not enough to reveal the dewy freshness of bourgeois love in *Romeo and Juliet*, its fatal empire-shattering drowsiness in *Antony and Cleopatra*, or the pageant of individual human wills in conflict in *Macbeth*, *Hamlet*, *Lear* and *Othello*. It was necessary to taste the dregs, to anticipate the era of *surréalisme* and James Joyce and write *Timon of Athens*, to express the degradation caused by the whole movement of capitalism, which sweeps away all feudal loyalties in order to realise the human spirit, only to find this spirit the miserable prisoner of the cash-nexus – to express this not symbolically, but with burning precision:

> Gold! yellow, glittering, precious gold! No, gods,
> I am no idle votarist. Roots, you clear heavens!
> Thus much of this will make black white, foul fair,
> Wrong right, base noble, old young, coward valiant.
> Ha! you gods, why this? What this, you gods? Why this
> Will lug your priests and servants from your sides,
> Pluck stout men's pillows from below their heads:
> This yellow slave
> Will knit and break religions; bless the accurs'd;
> Make the hoar leprosy ador'd; place thieves,
> And give them title, knee, and approbation,
> With senators on the bench; this is it
> That makes the wappen'd widow wed again;
> She, whom the spital-house and ulcerous sores
> Would cast the gorge at, this embalms and spices
> To the April day again. Come, damned earth,
> Thou common whore of mankind, that putt'st odds
> Among the rout of nations, I will make thee
> Do thy right nature.

James Joyce's characters repeat the experience of Timon:

> all is oblique,
> There's nothing level in our cursed natures
> But direct villainy. Therefore, be abhorred
> All feasts, societies, and throngs of men!
> His semblable, yea, *himself*, Timon disdains.
> Destruction, fang mankind!

From the life-thoughts of Elizabethan poetry to the death-thoughts of the age of imperialism is a tremendous period of development but all are comprehended and cloudily anticipated in Shakespeare's plays.

Before he died Shakespeare had cloudily and phantastically attempted an *un*tragic solution, a solution without death. Away from the rottenness of bourgeois civilisation, on the island of *The Tempest*, man attempts to live quietly and nobly, alone with his thoughts. Such an existence still retains an Elizabethan reality; there is an exploited class – Caliban, the bestial serf – and a 'free' spirit who serves only for a time – Ariel, apotheosis of the free wage-labourer. This heaven cannot endure. The actors return to the real world. The magic wand is broken. And yet, in its purity and childlike wisdom, there is a bewitching quality about *The Tempest* and its magic world, in which the forces of Nature are harnessed to men's service in a bizarre forecast of communism.

As primitive accumulation gradually generates a class of differentiated bourgeois producers, the will of the monarch, which in its absoluteness had been a creative force, now becomes anti-bourgeois and feudal. Once primitive accumulation has reached a certain point, what is urgently desired is not capital but a set of conditions in which the bourgeois can realise the development of his capital. This is the era of 'manufacture' – as opposed to factory development.

The absolute monarchy, by its free granting of monopolies and privileges, becomes as irksome as the old network of feudal loyalties. It is, after all, itself feudal. A cleavage appears between the monarchy and the class of artisans, merchants, farmers and shopkeepers.

The court supports the big landowner or noble who is already parasitic. He is allied with the court to exploit the bourgeoisie and the court rewards him with monopolies, privileges or special taxes which hamper the development of the overwhelming majority of the rising bourgeois class. Thus the absolute 'will' of the prince, now that the era of primitive accumulation is over, no longer expresses the life principle of the bourgeois class at this stage.

On the contrary the court appears as the source of evil. Its glittering corrupt life has a smell of decay; foulness and mean deeds are wrapped in silk. Bourgeois poetry changes into its opposite and by a unanimous movement puritanically draws its skirt's hem away from the dirt of the court life. The movement which at first was a reaction of the Reformed Church against the Catholic Church is now a reaction of the puritan against the Reformed Church.

The Church, expressing the absolute will of the monarch and the privileges of the nobility, is met by the individual 'conscience' of the puritan, which knows no law but the Spirit – his own will idealised. His thrift reflects the need, now that primitive accumulation is over, to amass the capital in which freedom and virtue inheres by 'saving' and not by gorgeous and extravagant robbery.

Donne expresses the transition, for he is torn by it. At first captivated by the sensuality and glittering brilliance of the court, the insolent treatment he receives produces a movement away from it, into repentance. The movement is not complete. In Donne's last years, filled as they are with death-thoughts and magniloquent hatred of life, the pride of the flesh still tears at his heart.

Poetry, drawing away from the collective life of the court, can only withdraw into the privacy of the bourgeois study, austerely furnished, shared only with a few friends, surroundings so different from the sleeping and waking publicity of court life that it rapidly revolutionises poetic technique. Crashaw, Herrick, Herbert, Vaughan – all the poetry of this era seems written by shy, proud men writing alone in their studies – appealing from court life to the country or to heaven. Language reflects the change. Lyrics no longer become something that a gentleman could sing to his lady; conceits are no longer something which could be tossed in courtly conversation. Poetry is no longer something to be roared out to a mixed audience. It smells of the library where it was produced. It is a learned man's poetry: student's poetry. Poetry is read, not declaimed: it is correspondingly subtle and intricate.

But Suckling and Lovelace write court poetry, the simple, open poetry of their class. They stand in antagonism to puritan poetry, and maintain the tradition of the Elizabethan court lyric.

The collective drama, born of the collective spirit of the court, necessarily perishes. Webster and Tourneur express the final corruption, the malignantly evil and Italianate death of the first stage of the bourgeois illusion.

The transitional period moves towards Revolution. The bourgeoisie revolt against the monarchy and the privileged nobility, in the name of Parliament, liberty and the 'Spirit' which is nothing but the bourgeois will challenging the monarchical. This is the era of armed revolution, of civil war, and with it emerges England's first openly revolutionary poet, Milton.

Revolutionary in style, revolutionary in content, the bourgeois now enters a stage of the illusion where he sees himself as defiant and lonely, challenging the powers that be. With this therefore goes an artificial and *consciously* noble style, an isolated style, the first of its kind in English poetry.

Bourgeois revolutions, which are only accomplished by the help of the people as a whole, always reach a stage where it is felt that they have 'gone too far'. The bourgeois demand for unlimited freedom is all very well until the 'have-nots' too demand unlimited freedom, which can only be obtained at the expense of the 'haves'. Then a Cromwell or Robespierre steps in to hold back coercively the progress of the Revolution.

Such a bourgeois halt must always lead to a reaction, for the bourgeois class thus destroys its own mass basis. A Robespierre gives place to a Directory and then a Napoleon; at an earlier stage, a Cromwell gives place to a Monk and a Charles II. The wheel does not come back full circle: there is a compromise.

To those who expressed directly the interests of the petty bourgeois, the puritans, this final stage of reaction is a betrayal of the Revolution. Therefore in *Paradise Lost* Milton sees himself as Satan overwhelmed and yet still courageous: damned and yet revolutionary. In *Paradise Regained* he has already rejected power in this world in exchange for power in the next. He scorns the temples and towers of this world; his reward is in the next because he will not compromise. Hence this poem is defeatist, and lacks the noble defiance of *Paradise Lost*. In *Samson Agonistes* Milton recovers his courage. He hopes for the day when he can pull the temple down on the luxury of his wanton oppressors and wipe out the Philistine court.

Did he consciously figure himself as Satan, Jesus and Samson? Only consciously perhaps as Samson. But when he came to tackle the bourgeois theme of how man, naturally good, is everywhere bad, and to give the familiar answer – because of Adam's fall from natural goodness as a result of temptation – he was led to consider the tempter, Satan and *his* fall. And Satan's struggle being plainly a revolution, he filled it with his revolutionary experience and made the defeated revolutionary a puritan, and the reactionary God a Stuart. Thus emerged the towering figure of Satan, which by its unexpected disproportion shows that Milton's theme had 'run away with him'.

In *Paradise Regained* Milton tries to believe that to be defeated temporally is to win spiritually, to win 'in the long run'. But Milton was a real, active revolutionary and in his heart he finds this spiritual satisfaction emptier than real defeat – as the unsatisfactoriness of the poem shows. In *Samson Agonistes* he tries to combine defeat and victory.

Of course the choice was already made in *Comus*, where the Lady spurns the luxury of the court and allies herself with the simple virtue of the people.

Note how already the bourgeois illusion is a little self-conscious. Milton is consciously noble – Shakespeare never. The Elizabethans are heroic: the Puritans are not, and therefore have to see themselves as heroic, in an archaistic dress. The verse and vocabulary of the Latin secretary to the Provisional Government well expresses this second movement of the illusion. The theme of the poems cannot at once be noble and in any sense contemporary. Poetry is already isolating itself from the collective daily life, which makes it inevitable that the prose 'story' now begins to appear as an opposite pole.

Of course the transition from the court, like all other movements of the bourgeois illusion, is foreshadowed in Shakespeare. In *The Tempest* Prospero withdraws from corrupt court life to the peace of his island study, like a Herbert or a Milton. Shakespeare did the same in life when he retired to Stratford-on-Avon.

But he could not write there. His magic wand was a collective one. He had broken it with the breaking of his tie with the court, and the cloud-capp'd palaces of his fancy became empty air.

The atmosphere of a period of reaction such as that which followed the Puritan Revolution is of good-humoured cynicism. A betrayal of the extreme 'ideals' for which the battle had been fought appeared prudent to the majority. Unrestrained liberty and the free following of the spirit, excellent in theory, had in practice been proved to involve awkwardnesses for the very class of whom it was the battle-cry. The bourgeois illusion went through a new stage, that of the Restoration.

Such a movement is cynical, because it is the outcome of a betrayal of 'ideals' for earthly reasons. It is luxurious because the class with whom the bourgeoisie, having taught it a sharp lesson, now allies itself again – the landed nobility – has no need of thrift to acquire capital. It is collective because there is a return to the public court life and the play. It is not decadent in any real sense; true, the bourgeoisie has allied itself with the old doomed class – but it has breathed new life into that class. Webster, expressing the decadence of the court, gives way to Dryden, expressing its vigour. And Dryden, with his turncoat life, so different from Milton's rectitude, exactly expresses the confused and rapid movement of the bourgeoisie of the time, from Cromwell to Charles II and from James II to William III. It is a real alliance – there is no question of the feudal regime returning. James II's fate in the 'Glorious Revolution' clearly shows the bourgeoisie have come to rule.

The poet must return from his study to court, but it is now a more cityfied, sensible, less romantic and picturesque court. The court itself has become almost burgher. The language shows the same passage from study to London street, from conscious heroism to business-like common sense. The sectarian bourgeois revolutionary, a little inclined to pose, becomes the sensible man-of-the-world. This is the transition from Milton to Dryden. The idealisation of compromise between rival classes as 'order' and 'measure' – a familiar feature of reaction – leads to the conception of the Augustan age, which passes by an inevitable transition into eighteenth-century nationalism, once the Glorious Revolution has shown that the bourgeoisie are dominant in the alliance.

The self-valuation of this age as Augustan is in fact singularly fitting. Caesar played the role of Cromwell, and Augustus of Charles II in a similar movement in Rome, where the knightly class at first rebelled against the senatorial and, when it became dangerous to go farther, entered on a road of compromise and reaction.

Elizabethan insurgence, the voice of primitive accumulation, thus turns into its opposite, Augustan propriety, the voice of manufacture. Individualism gives place to good taste. In its early stages bourgeoisdom requires the shattering of all feudal forms, and therefore its illusion is a realisation of the instincts in freedom. In the course of this movement, first to acquire capital, and then to give capital free play, it leans first on the monarchy – Shakespeare – and then on the common people – Milton. But because it is the interests of a class, it dare not go too far in its claims, for to advance the interests of all society is to deny its own. It must not only shatter the old forms which maintained the rule of the feudal class, but it must create the new forms which will ensure its own development as a ruling class. This is the epoch of manufacture and of agricultural capitalism. Land, not factories, is still the pivot.

This epoch is not only opposed to that of primitive accumulation, it is also opposed to that of free trade. Capital exists, but the proletariat is as yet barely in existence. The numerous artisans and peasants are not yet proletarianised by the very movement of capital: the State must therefore be invoked to assist the process. The expansive period of capitalism, in which the rapid expropriation of the artisan hurls thousands of free labourers on to the market, has not yet arrived. The vagrants of Elizabethan days have already been absorbed. The bourgeoisie finds that there is a shortage of wage-labour which might lead to a rise in the price of labour-power over and above its value (i.e. its cost of reproduction in food and rent).

Hence there is need for a network of laws to keep down wages and prices and regulate labour in order to secure for the bourgeois class the conditions of its development. It now sees the 'impracticable idealism' of its revolutionary demands for liberty. Order, measure, law, good taste and other imposed forms are necessary. Tradition and convention are valuable. Now that the feudal State has perished, these restraints ensure the development of bourgeois economy. Free trade seems the very opposite of desirable to the economists of this era. The bourgeois illusion betrays itself.

Therefore, during the eighteenth century, bourgeois poetry expresses the spirit of manufacture, of the petty manufacturing bourgeoisie, beneath the wings of the big landowning capitalists, giving birth to industrial capitalism. The shattering expansion of capitalism has not yet begun. Capitalism still approximates to those economies where 'conservation is the first condition of existence' and has not yet fully entered into the state where it 'cannot exist without constantly revolutionising the means of production'. Capitalism is revolutionising itself, but like a slowly growing plant that needs protection, instead of like an explosion in which the ignition of one part detonates the rest. By the compromise of the Glorious Revolution, the Whig landed aristocracy were prepared to give that protection because they had themselves become bourgeoisified.

It was only when the separation between agricultural and industrial capitalism took place as a result of the rise of the factory that the cleavage between the aristocracy and the bourgeoisie began to have a determining effect on the bourgeois illusion. While the woollen-mill was still no more than a hand-loom and an appendage of the agricultural capitalist's sheep-farm there was no direct antagonism between the classes: it was only as the woollen-mill became a cotton-mill, depending for its raw material on outside sources, and when sheep-farming developed in Australia and provided wool for English mills, that there arose a direct antagonism between agricultural and industrial capitalism which expressed itself ultimately on the side of the industrialists as a demand for Free Trade and the repeal of the Corn Laws.

Pope's poetry, and its 'reason' – a reason moving within singularly simple and shallow categories but moving accurately – with its polished language and metre and curt antitheses, is a reflection of that stage of the bourgeois illusion where freedom for the bourgeoisie can only be 'limited' – man must be prudent in his demands, and yet there is no reason for despair, all goes well. Life is on the up-grade, but it is impossible to hurry. The imposition of outward forms on the heart is necessary and accepted. Hence the contrast between the elegant corset of the eighteenth-century heroic couplet and the natural luxuriance of Elizabethan blank verse, whose sprawl almost conceals the bony structure of the iambic rhythm inside it.

Pope perfectly expresses the ideals of the bourgeois class in alliance with a bourgeoisified aristocracy in the epoch of manufacture.

It is important to note that even now the poet himself has not been bourgeoisified as a producer. He does not produce as yet for the free market. Almost a court or aristocratic official in the time of Shakespeare, poet is a parson's or scholar's occupation in the ensuing period, and even as late as Pope he is dependent on being patronised, i.e. he has a 'patriarchal' or 'idyllic' relation to the class of whom he is the spokesman in the time of Pope.

Such an 'idyllic' relation means that the poet writes non-idyllic poetry. He still sees himself as a man playing a social role. This was the case with the primitive poet; it remains true of Pope. It imposes on him the obligation to speak the language of his paymasters or co-poets – in the primitive tribe these constitute the whole tribe, in Augustan society these are the men who form his patron's circle – the ruling class. Johnson – dependent on subscribers – bridges the gap between the poet by status and the poet as producer. Thus poetry remains in this sense collective. It talks a more or less current language, and the poet writes for an audience he has directly in mind, to whom perhaps he will presently read his poems and so be able to watch their effect. Poetry is still for him not so much a poem – a self-subsisting work of art – as a movement from writer to reader, like the movement of emotion in a publicly acted drama or the movement of a Muse in the minds of men. Hence he realises himself as playing a social role: inspirer of humanity or redresser of the follies of mankind. He has not yet become a self-conscious artist.

8

English Poets II:
The Industrial Revolution

The bourgeois illusion now passes to another stage, that of the Industrial Revolution, the 'explosive' stage of capitalism. Now the growth of capitalism transforms all idyllic patriarchal relations – including that of the poet to the class whose aspirations he voices – into 'callous' cash-nexus.

Of course this does not make the poet regard himself as a shop-keeper and his poems as cheeses. To suppose this is to overlook the compensatory and dynamic nature of the connection between illusion and reality. In fact it has the opposite effect. It has the effect of making the poet increasingly regard himself as a man removed from society, as an individualist realising only the instincts of his heart and not responsible to society's demands, whether expressed in the duties of a citizen, a fearer of God or a faithful servant of Mammon. At the same time his poems come increasingly to seem worthy ends-in-themselves.

This is the final explosive movement of the bourgeois contradiction. The bourgeois illusion has already swayed from antithesis to antithesis, but as a result of this last final movement it can only pass, like a whirling piece of metal thrown off by an exploding flywheel, out of the orbit of the bourgeois categories of thought altogether.

As a result of the compromise of the eighteenth century, beneath the network of safeguards and protections which was characteristic of the era of manufacture, bourgeois economy developed to the stage where by the use of the machine, the steam-engine and the power-loom it acquired an enormous power of self-expansion. At the same time the 'factory' broke away from the farm, of which it was the handicraft adjunct and challenged it as a mightier and opposed force.

On the one hand organised labour inside the factory progressively increased, on the other hand the individual anarchy of the external market also increased. On the one hand there was an increasingly public form of production, on the other hand an increasingly private form of appropriation. At the one pole was an increasingly landless and tool-less proletariat, at the other an increasingly wealthy bourgeoisie. This self-contradiction in capitalist economy provided the terrific momentum of the Industrial Revolution.

The bourgeoisie, who had found its own revolutionary-puritan ideals of liberty 'extreme', and returned to the compromise of mercantilist good taste that seemed eternal reason, now again found its heart had been right, and reason wrong.

This revealed itself first of all as a cleavage between the former landed aristocracy and the industrial bourgeoisie, expressing the rise of the factory to predominance over the farm. The landed aristocracy, and the restrictions it demanded for its growth, was now confronted by industrial capital and its demands. Capital had found an inexhaustible self-expansive power in machinery and outside sources of raw material. So far from any of the earlier forms being of value to it, they were so many restraints. The cost of labour-power could safely be left to fall to its real value, for the machine by its competition creates the proletariat it requires to serve it. The real value of labour-power in turn depends on the real value of wheat, which is less in the colonies and America than in England because there it embodies less socially necessary labour. The Corn Laws, which safeguard the agricultural capitalist, therefore hamper the industrialist. Their interests – reconciled during the period of wage-labour shortage – are now opposed. All the forms and restraints that oppose this free expansion of the industrial bourgeoisie must be shattered. To accomplish this shattering, the bourgeoisie called to its standard all other classes, precisely as in the time of the Puritan Revolution. It claimed to speak for the people as against the oppressors. It demanded Reform and the Repeal of the Corn Laws. It attacked the Church, either as Puritan (Methodist) or as open sceptic. It attacked all laws as restrictive of equality. It advanced the conception of the naturally good man, born free but everywhere in chains. Such revolts against existing systems of laws, canons, forms and traditions always appear as a revolt of the heart against reason, a revolt of feeling and the sentiments against sterile formalism and the tyranny of the past. Marlowe, Shelley, Lawrence and Dali have a certain parallelism here; each expresses this revolt in a manner appropriate to the period.

We cannot understand this final movement of poetry unless we understand that at every step the bourgeois is revolutionary in that he is revolutionising his own basis. But he revolutionises it only to make it consistently more bourgeois. In the same way, each important bourgeois poet is revolutionary, but he expresses the very movement which brings more violently into the open the contradiction against which his revolutionary poetry is a protest. They are 'mirror revolutionaries'. They attempt to reach an object in a mirror, only to move farther away from the real object. And what can that object be but the common object of man as producer and as poet – freedom? The poignancy of their tragedy and pessimism derives its bite from this perpetual recession of the desired object as they advance to grasp it. 'La Belle Dame Sans Merci' has them all in thrall. They wake up on the cold hillside.

Blake, Byron, Keats, Wordsworth and Shelley express this ideological revolution, each in their different ways, as a Romantic Revolution.

Byron is an aristocrat – but he is one who is conscious of the break-up of his class as a force, and the necessity to go over to the bourgeoisie. Hence his mixture of cynicism and romanticism.

These deserters are in moments of revolution always useful and always dangerous allies. Too often their desertion of their class and their attachment to another, is not so much a 'comprehension of the historical movement as a whole' as a revolt against the cramping circumstances imposed on them by their own class's dissolution, and in a mood of egoistic anarchy they seize upon the aspirations of the other class as a weapon in their private battle. They are always individualistic, romantic figures with a strong element of the *poseur*. They will the destruction of their own class but not the rise of the other, and this rise, when it becomes evident and demands that they change their merely destructive enmity to the dying class to a constructive loyalty to the new, may, in act if not in word, throw them back into the arms of the enemy. They become counter-revolutionaries. Danton and Trotsky are examples of this type. Byron's death at Missolonghi occurred before any such complete development, but it is significant that he was prepared to fight for liberty in Greece rather than England. In him the revolt of the heart against the reason appears as the revolt of the hero against circumstances, against morals, against all 'pettiness' and convention. This Byronism is very symptomatic, and it is also symptomatic that in Byron it goes with a complete selfishness and carelessness for the sensibilities of others. Milton's Satan has taken on a new guise, one far less noble, petulant even.

Byron is most successful as a mocker – as a Don Juan. On the one hand to be cynical, to mock at the farce of human existence, on the other hand to be sentimental, and complain of the way in which the existing society has tortured one's magnificent capabilities – that is the essence of Byronism. It represents the demoralisation in the ranks of the aristocracy as much as a rebellion against the aristocracy. These men are therefore always full of death-thoughts: the death-thoughts of Fascism fighting in the last ditch, the death-thoughts of Jacobites; the glorification of a heroic death justifying a more dubious life. The same secret death-wishes are shown by these aristocrats if they turn revolutionary, performing deeds of outstanding individual heroism – sometimes unnecessary, sometimes useful, but always romantic and single-handed. They cannot rise beyond the conception of the desperate hero of revolution.

Shelley, however, expresses a far more genuinely dynamic force. He speaks for the bourgeoisie who, at this stage of history, feel themselves the dynamic force of society and therefore voice demands not merely for themselves but for the whole of suffering humanity. It seems to them that if only *they* could realise themselves, that is, bring into being the conditions necessary for their own freedom, this would of itself ensure the freedom of all. Shelley believes that he speaks for all men, for all sufferers, calls them all to a brighter future. The bourgeois trammelled by the restraints of the era of mercantilism is Prometheus, bringer of fire, fit symbol of the machine-wielding capitalist. Free him and the world is free. A Godwinist, Shelley believed that man is naturally good – institutions debase him. Shelley is the most revolutionary of the bourgeois poets of this era because *Prometheus Unbound* is not an excursion into the past, but a revolutionary programme for the present. It tallies with Shelley's own intimate participation in the bourgeois-democratic revolutionary movement of his day.

Although Shelley is an atheist, he is not a materialist. He is an idealist. His vocabulary is, for the first time, consciously idealist – that is, full of words like 'brightness', 'truth', 'beauty', 'soul', 'aether', 'wings', 'fainting', 'panting' – which stir a whole world of indistinct emotions. Such complexes, because of their numerous emotional associations, appear to make the word indicate one distinct concrete entity, although in fact no such entity exists, but each word denotes a variety of different concepts.

This idealism is a reflection of the revolutionary bourgeois belief that, once the existing social relations that hamper a human being are shattered, the 'natural man will be realised' – his feelings, his emotions, his aspirations, will all be immediately bodied forth as material realities. Shelley does not see that these shattered social relations can only give place to the social relations of the class strong enough to shatter them and that in any case these feelings, aspirations and emotions are the product of the social relations in which he exists and that to realise them a social act is necessary, which in turn has its effect upon a man's feelings, aspirations and emotions.

The bourgeois illusion is, in the sphere of poetry, a revolt. In Wordsworth the revolt takes the form of a return to the natural man, just as it does in Shelley. Wordsworth, like Shelley profoundly influenced by French Rousseauism, seeks freedom, beauty – all that is not now in man because of his social relations – in 'Nature'. The French Revolution now intervenes. The bourgeois demand for freedom has now a regressive tinge. It no longer looks forward to freedom by revolt but by return to the natural man.

Wordsworth's 'Nature' is of course a Nature freed of wild beasts and danger by aeons of human work, a Nature in which the poet, enjoying a comfortable income, lives on the products of industrialism even while he enjoys the natural scene 'unspoilt' by industrialism. The very division of industrial capitalism from agricultural capitalism has now separated the country from the town. The division of labour involved in industrialism has made it possible for sufficient surplus produce to exist to maintain a poet in austere idleness in Cumberland. But to see the relation between the two, to see that the culture, gift of language and leisure which distinguish a Nature poet from a dumb sub-human are the product of economic activity – to see this would be to pierce the bourgeois illusion and expose the artificiality of 'Nature' poetry. Such poetry can only arise at a time when man by industrialism has mastered Nature – but not himself.

Wordsworth therefore is a pessimist. Unlike Shelley, he revolts regressively – but still in a bourgeois way – by demanding freedom from social relations, the specific social relations of industrialism, while still retaining the products, the freedom, which these relations alone make possible.

With this goes a theory that 'natural', i.e. *conversational*, language is better, and therefore more poetic than 'artificial', i.e. *literary*, language. He does not see that both are equally artificial – i.e. directed to a social end – and equally natural, i.e. products of man's struggle with Nature. They merely represent different spheres and stages of that struggle and are good or bad not in themselves, but in relation to this struggle. Under the spell of this theory some of Wordsworth's worst poetry is written.

Wordsworth's form of the bourgeois illusion has some kinship with Milton's. Both exalt the natural man, one in the form of Puritan 'Spirit', the other in the more sophisticated form of pantheistic 'Nature'. One appeals to the primal Adam as proof of man's natural innocence, the other to the primal child. In the one case original sin, in the other social relations, account for the fall from grace. Both therefore are at their best when consciously noble and elevated. Milton, reacting against primitive accumulation and its deification of naive princely desire and will, does not, however – as Wordsworth does glorify the wild element in man, the natural primitive. Hence he is saved from a technical theory that conduces to 'sinking' in poetry.

Keats is the first great poet to feel the strain of the poet's position in this stage of the bourgeois illusion, as producer for the free market. Wordsworth has a small income; Shelley, although always in want, belongs to a rich family and his want is due simply to carelessness, generosity and the impracticability which is often the reaction of certain temperaments to a wealthy home. But Keats comes of a small bourgeois family and is always pestered by money problems. The sale of his poems is an important consideration to him.

For Keats therefore freedom does not lie, like Wordsworth, in a return to Nature; his returns to Nature were always accompanied by the uncomfortable worry, where was the money coming from? It could not lie, as with Shelley, in a release from the social relations of this world, for mere formal liberty would still leave the individual with the problem of earning a living. Keats' greater knowledge of bourgeois reality therefore led him to a position which was to set the keynote for future bourgeois poetry: 'revolution' as a flight *from* reality. Keats is the bannerbearer of the Romantic Revival. The poet now escapes upon the 'rapid wings of poesy' to a world of romance, beauty and sensuous life separate from the poor, harsh, real world of everyday life, which it sweetens and by its own loveliness silently condemns.

This world is the shadowy enchanted world built by Lamia for her lover or by the Moon for Endymion. It is the golden-gated upper world of Hyperion, the word-painted lands of the nightingale, of the Grecian urn, of Baiae's isle. This other world is defiantly counterposed to the real world.

'Beauty is truth, truth beauty' – that is all
Ye know on earth, and all ye need to know.

And always it is threatened by stern reality in the shape of sages, rival powers or the drab forces of everyday. Isabella's world of love is shattered by the two money-grubbing brothers. Even the wild loveliness of *The Eve of St. Agnes* is a mere interlude between storm and storm, a coloured dream snatched from the heart of cold and darkness – the last stanzas proclaim the triumph of decay. 'La Belle Dame Sans Merci' gives her knight only a brief delight before he wakes. The flowering basil sprouts from the rotting head of Isabella's lover, and is watered with her tears.

The fancy cannot cheat so well
As she is famed to do, deceiving elf! ...
Was it a vision or a waking dream?
Fled is that music – do I wake or sleep?

Like Cortez, Keats gazes entranced at the New World of poetry, Chapman's realms of gold, summoned into being to redress the balance of the old, but however much voyaged in, it is still only a world of fancy.

A new vocabulary emerges with Keats, the dominating vocabulary of future poetry. Not Wordsworth's – because the appeal is not to the unspoilt simplicity of the country. Not Shelley's – because the appeal is not to the 'ideas' that float on the surface of real material life and can be skimmed off like froth. The country is a part of the real material world, and the froth of these metaphysical worlds is too unsubstantial and therefore is always a reminder of the real world which generated it. A world must be constructed which is more real precisely because it is more unreal and has sufficient inner stiffness to confront the real world with the self-confidence of a successful conjuring trick.

Instead of taking, like Wordsworth and Shelley, what is regarded as the most natural, spiritual or beautiful part of the real world, a new world is built up out of words, as by a mosaic artist, and these words therefore must have solidity and reality. The Keatsian vocabulary is full of words with a hard material texture, like tesserae, but it is an 'artificial' texture – all crimson, scented, archaic, stiff, jewelled and anti-contemporary. It is as vivid as missal painting. Increasingly this world is set in the world of feudalism, but it is not a feudal world. It is a bourgeois world – the world of the Gothic cathedrals and all the growing life and vigour of the bourgeois class under late feudalism. Here too poetic revolution has a strong regressive character, just as it had with Wordsworth, but had not with the most genuinely revolutionary poet, Shelley.

The bourgeois, with each fresh demand he makes for individualism, free competition, absence of social relations and more equality, only brings to birth greater organisation, more complex social relations, higher degrees of trustification and combination, more inequality. Yet each of these contradictory movements revolutionises his basis and creates new productive forces. In the same way the bourgeois revolution, expressed in the poetry of Shelley, Wordsworth and Keats, although it is contradictory in its movement, yet brings into being vast new technical resources for poetry and revolutionises the whole apparatus of the art.

The basic movement is in many ways parallel to the movement of primitive accumulation which gave rise to Elizabethan poetry. Hence there was at this era among poets a revival of interest in Shakespeare and the Elizabethans. The insurgent outburst of the genetic individuality which is expressed in Elizabethan poetry had a collective guise, because it was focused on that collective figure, the prince. In romantic poetry it has a more artificial air as an expression of the sentiments and the emotions of the individual figure, the 'independent' bourgeois. Poetry has separated itself from the story, the heart from the intellect, the individual from society; all is more artificial, differentiated and complex.

The poet now begins to show the marks of commodity production. We shall analyse this still further when, as in a later date, it sets the whole key for poetry. At present the most important sign is Keats' statement, that he could write for ever, burning his poems afterwards. The poem has become already an end in itself.

But it is more important to note the air of tragedy that from now on looms over all bourgeois poetry that is worth the adjective 'great'. Poetry has become pessimistic and self-lacerating. Byron, Keats and Shelley die young. And though it is usual to regret that they died with their best works unwritten, the examples of Wordsworth, Swinburne and Tennyson make fairly clear that this is not the case, that the personal tragedy of their deaths, which in the case of Shelley and Byron at least seemed sought, prevented the tragedy of the bourgeois illusion working itself out impersonally in their poetry. For the contradiction which secures the movement of capitalism was now unfolding so rapidly that it exposed itself in the lifetime of a poet and always in the same way. The ardent hopes, the aspirations, the faiths of the poet's youth melted or else were repeated in the face of a changed reality with a stiffness and sterility that betrayed the lack of conviction and made them a mocking caricature of their youthful sincerity. True, all men grow old and lose their youthful hopes – but not in this way. A middle-aged Sophocles can speak with searching maturity of the tragedy of his life, and at eighty he writes a drama that reflects the open-eyed serenity of wisdom's child grown aged. But mature bourgeois poets are not capable of tragedy or resignation, only of a dull repetition of the faiths of youth – or silence. The movement of history betrays the contradiction for what it is and yet forces the bourgeois to cling to it. From that moment the lie has entered his soul, and by shutting his eyes to the consciousness of necessity, he has delivered his soul to slavery.

In the French Revolution, the bourgeoisie, in the name of liberty, equality and fraternity, revolted against obsolete social relations. They claimed, like Shelley, to speak in the name of all mankind; but then arose, at first indistinctly, later with continually increasing clarity, the claim of the proletariat also demanding liberty, equality and fraternity. But to grant these to the proletariat means the abolition of the very conditions which secure the existence of the bourgeois class and the exploitation of the proletariat. Therefore the movement for freedom, which at first speaks largely in the voice of mankind, is always halted at a state where the bourgeoisie must betray its ideal structure expressed in poetry, forget that it claimed to speak for humanity, and crush the class whose like demands are irreconcilable with its own existence. Once robbed of its mass support, the revolting bourgeoisie can always be beaten back a stage by the forces of reaction. True, these forces have learned 'a sharp lesson' and do not proceed too far against the bourgeoisie who have shown their power. Both ally themselves against the proletariat. Ensues an equilibrium when the bourgeoisie have betrayed their talk of freedom, and compromised their ideal structure, only themselves to have lost part of the ideal fruit of their struggle to the more reactionary forces – feudal forces, if the struggle is against feudalism, landowning and big financial forces, if the struggle is between agricultural and industrial capitalism.

Such a movement was that from Robespierre to the Directory and the anti-Jacobin movement which as a result of the French Revolution swept Europe everywhere. The whole of the nineteenth century is a record of the same betrayal, which in the life of the poets expresses itself as a betrayal of youthful idealism; 1830, 1848 and, finally, 1871 are the dates which make all bourgeois poets now tread the path of Wordsworth, whose revolutionary fire, as the result of the proletarian content of the final stage of the French Revolution, was suddenly chilled and gave place to common sense, respectability and piety.

It was Keats who wrote:

'None can usurp this height', the shade returned,
'Save those to whom the misery of the world
Is misery and will not let them rest.'

The doom of bourgeois poets in this epoch is precisely that the misery of the world, including their own special misery, will not let them rest, and yet the temper of the time forces them to support the class which causes it. The proletarian revolution has not yet advanced to a stage where 'some bourgeois ideologists, comprehending the historical movement as a whole', can ally themselves with it and really speak for suffering humanity and for a class which is the majority now and the whole world of men tomorrow. They speak only for a class that is creating the world of tomorrow willy-nilly, and at each step draws back and betrays its instinctive aspirations because of its conscious knowledge that this world of tomorrow it is creating, *cannot include itself*.

9

English Poets III:
The Decline of Capitalism

* * *

Just as the growth of capitalism tends more and more to whelm all industrial production in mass production, expropriate artisans in thousands, and proletarianise the craftsman to the level of a labourer or machine-minder, so it has the same effect in the realm of art. Mass-production art enforces a dead level of mediocrity. Good art becomes less saleable. Because art's role is now that of adapting the multitude to the dead mechanical existence of capitalist production, in which work sucks them of their vital energies without awakening their instincts, where leisure becomes a time to deaden the mind with the easy phantasy of films, simple wish-fulfilment writing, or music that is mere emotional massage – because of this the paid craft of writer becomes as tedious and wearisome as that of machine-minder. Journalism becomes the characteristic product of the age. Films, the novel and painting all share in the degradation. Immense technical resources and steady debasement and stereotyping of the human psyche are characteristics alike of factory production and factory art in this stage of capitalism. Let any artist who has had to earn a living by journalism or writing 'thrillers' testify to the inexorable proletarianisation of his art. The modern thriller, love story, cowboy romance, cheap film, jazz music or yellow Sunday paper form the real *proletarian* literature of today – that is, literature which is the characteristic accompaniment of the misery and instinctual poverty produced in the majority of people by modern capitalist production. It is literature which proletarianises the writer. It is at once an expression of real misery and a protest against that real misery. This art, universal, constant, fabulous, full of the easy gratifications of instincts starved by modern capitalism, peopled by passionate lovers and heroic cowboys and amazing detectives, is the religion of today, as characteristic an expression of proletarian exploitation as Catholicism is of feudal exploitation. It is the opium of the people; it pictures an inverted world because the world of society *is* inverted. It is the real characteristic art of bourgeois civilisation, expressing the real and not the self-appraised content of the bourgeois illusion. 'High-brow' bourgeois art grows on the bourgeois class's freedom. 'Low-brow' proletarian art grows on the proletariat's unfreedom and helps, by its massage of the starved revolting instincts, to maintain that unfreedom in being. Because it is mere massage, because it helps to maintain man in unfreedom and not to express his spontaneous creation, because of that, it is bad art. Yet it is an art which is far more really characteristic, which plays a far more important and all-pervasive role in bourgeois society than, for example, the art of James Joyce.

The poet is the most craft of writers. His art requires the highest degree of technical skill of any artist; and it is precisely this technical skill which is not wanted by the vast majority of people in a developed capitalism. He is as out of date as a medieval stone-carver in an era of plaster casts. As the virtual proletarianisation of society increases, the conditions of men's work, robbed of spontaneity, more and more make them demand a mass-produced 'low-brow' art, whose flatness and shallowness serve to adapt them to their unfreedom. The poet becomes a 'high-brow', a man whose skill is not wanted. It becomes too much trouble for the average man to read poetry.

Because of the conditions of his life, the poet's reaction is similar to that of the craftsman. He begins to set craft skill in *opposition* to social function, 'art' in opposition to 'life'. The craftsman's particular version of commodity-fetishism is *skill-fetishism*. Skill now seems an objective thing, opposed to social value. The art work therefore becomes valued in and for itself.

But the art work lives in a world of society. Art works are always composed of objects that have a social reference. Not mere noises but words from a vocabulary, not chance sounds but notes from a socially recognised scale, not mere blobs but forms with a *meaning*, are what constitutes the material of art. All these things have emotional associations which are social.

Yet if an art work is valued for *its own sake* in defiant and rebellious opposition to the sake of a society which now has no use for skill, it is in fact valued *for the artist's sake*. One cannot simply construct random poems. If their associations are not social they are personal, and the more the art work is opposed to society, the more are personal associations defiantly selected which are exclusive of social ones – bizarre, strange, phantastic. In this stage of the bourgeois illusion therefore, poetry exhibits a rapid movement from the social world of art to the personal world of private phantasy. This leads to individualism. In revolting against capitalism the poet, because he remains within the sphere of bourgeois categories, simply moves on to an extreme individualism, utter 'loss of control of his social relationships', and absolute commodity production – to the essence, in fact, of the capitalism he condemns. He is the complete mirror revolutionary.

And his too triumphant proclamation of liberty at last achieved in full, marks the very moment when liberty completely slips out of his hands.

*　*　*

At each stage the bourgeois contradiction by unfolding itself revolutionises its own base and secures a fresh development of technical resources. Hence the movement from 'art for art's sake' to *surréalisme* secures a development of the technique of poetry, of which in England Eliot is the best example owing to the already mentioned lag. But it cannot continue indefinitely. The conflict between technical resources and content reaches a limit where it explodes and begins to turn into its opposite. A revolution of content, as opposed to a mere movement of technique, now begins, corresponding in the social sphere to a change in productive relations as opposed to a mere improvement in productive forces. As a result the social associations of words will all be re-cast, and the whole subject-matter of poetry will become different, because language itself is now generated in a different society. There will be a really revolutionary movement from the categories of bourgeois poetry to the categories of communist poetry.

The *surréaliste* therefore is the last bourgeois revolutionary. To pass beyond him – beyond Milton, beyond Godwin, beyond Pater, beyond finally Dada and Dali, is to pass beyond the categories of bourgeois thought. What politically is this final bourgeois revolutionary? He is an anarchist.

The anarchist is a bourgeois so disgusted with the development of bourgeois society that he asserts the bourgeois creed in the most essential way: complete 'personal' freedom, complete destruction of all social relations. The anarchist is yet revolutionary because he represents the destructive element and the complete negation of all bourgeois society. But he cannot really pass beyond bourgeois society, because he remains caught in its toils. In the anarchic organisation of bourgeois economy, certain laws of organisation still assert themselves, and therefore can only be shattered by a higher organisation, that of a new ruling class.

* * *

In a country such as England, the final revolt of the craftsman usually takes a different form. The craftsman is not there an independent artisan or petty bourgeois whose first taste of proletarianisation gives him a hatred of 'organisation'. The proletarianisation of the artisan took place in the late eighteenth century in England, and because the possibilities of revolution were more hopeless, his rebellion took the form of Ludditism – the smashing of the machines which expropriated them. The next great proletarianisation of the craftsman was marked by the rise of the general labourers' unions in the face of the opposition of the craft unions, and the struggle then was a struggle between a developing proletariat and the capitalists, with the craft unions standing aside.

Thus the final crisis in England found the craftsman a man who, as the result of the long springtime of English capitalist development, occupied a privileged position in production. He formed the famous labour aristocracy who made it seem as if England, not content with a bourgeois aristocracy and a bourgeois monarchy, aimed also at a bourgeois proletariat. In the final crisis it soon became apparent that this favoured position was only the expression of the temporary supremacy of England in world capitalism and vanished with the growth of competition and tariffs. Unemployment, insecurity, wage-cuts and dismissals as the result of rationalisation, from 1929 to 1936, ravaged all the ranks of the 'craft' and 'professional' elements of England just as, at a somewhat earlier date, they had those of Germany. So far, however, from proletarianisation in all cases producing an anarchic frame of mind in these types, it has an opposite effect in those who are 'key' men rooted in the heart of industry everywhere – in the tool-room of the factory, as supervisors, foremen, technicians, specialists, managers and consultants. In these positions they find that their skill is wasted, not by the organisation of men into factories, but because the progress of this organisation – its logical conclusion in an immensely increased human productivity – is defeated by the characteristic anarchy of capitalist production – the individual ownership and mutual competition of the various factories.

Hence their revolution against the system which is crippling them is not reactionary in content, like the artisan's, but genuinely progressive, in that it demands greater organisation – the extension of the organisation already obtaining in the factories to production as a whole.

But though progressive in content, it by no means follows that this demand will find an outcome in a progressive act. Even at this revolutionary stage the craftsman halts at two paths. One leads up to the bourgeoisie with whom his responsible position and higher salary have always associated him – indeed the doctor, architect, and artist, owing to the 'ideal' content of their work, have actually been a genuine part of the bourgeoisie. The other path leads downward to the proletariat, from whom his privileged position has always sundered him – for proletarianisation, because it has involved worsened living conditions, has been something to be avoided at all costs. Hence he has an ingrained repulsion from alliance with the proletariat. In the past he has measured his success and freedom by the distance he has climbed up from the proletariat to the bourgeoisie – the famous petty bourgeois snobbery and exclusiveness which is only the cold reflection of man's constant desire for freedom.

If he chooses the upward path, he chooses organisation imposed from above by the bourgeoisie – in other words, Fascism. Of course this organisation is a mere sham – it is a cloak for further rationalisation, and the consolidating of the power of the most reactionary section of the capitalist class. It results, not in the increased organisation of production but in greater anarchy and more bitter competition. Rationalisation is in fact irrationalisation. It leads to an increase in anarchy outside and inside – internally by a profound disturbance in economy resulting from the growth of armament and luxury industry at the expense of necessities and a general lowering of wages, and externally by an increase in tariffs and imperialism and a general drive towards war. The only real organisation consists in the counter-revolutionary regimentation of the proletariat and petty bourgeois classes and the smashing of working-class organisations.

But equally the craftsman may choose the downward path, and he is the more likely to do so as the development of the industrial crisis and the objective examples of Fascism abroad reveal the inevitability of this move. This path consists of allying himself with the proletariat and extending the organisation of the workers within the factories to the organisation of production as a whole by liquidating those rights which stand in the way – individual ownership of the means of production. Since this right is the real power of existing society, this means the substitution of workers' power for capitalists' power. When he makes this choice, the craftsman, because of his key position in production, his privileged income (giving him more leisure and cultural opportunities), and his experience of responsibility, becomes a natural leader of the proletariat, instead of their most treacherous enemy, as he is when he is allied with the bourgeoisie.

It is for this reason that the last three years in England have been marked by the development of a revolutionary outlook among those very craft and petty bourgeois types – the 'labour aristocracy' – who formerly displayed all the reactionary qualities that made a craft union notorious in this country and made many of their spokesmen in Germany actual supporters of the Fascist regime. Anyone familiar with trade union affairs is aware that just as the craft unions and those industrial unions with a strong craft composition formerly opposed the general labourers' unions as being too militant and 'socialist', it is now the craft and semi-professional unions like the A.E.U., E.T.U., A.S.L.E. & F., N.A.U.S.W. & C. and N.U.C. who at the Trades Union Congress and through their branches and Metropolitan Councils or District Committees press for militant action and are reproached by the general unions for being too extreme and communist. In the same way those craftsmen whose ideal theoretical content has given them a special position among the bourgeoisie itself – doctors, scientists, architects and teachers – are now moving Left and entering the Communist Party in considerable numbers, passing straight from Liberalism without an intermediate sojourn in the Labour Party.

The same final movement of the bourgeois illusion is reflected in the growth of the People's Front, where all the liberal elements, representing the craft content of modern society, put themselves under the leadership of the proletariat in a formal written alliance limiting the scope of that leadership.

In English poetry this is reflected in the fact that English poets, without ever moving completely into *surréaliste* anarchy, change from a position near *surréalisme* into its opposite – a communist revolutionary position, such as that adopted by Auden, Lewis, Spender and Lehmann. How far this is genuinely communist and what level of art it represents, is a consideration which will be deferred to our final chapter, for with this movement the bourgeois contradiction passes into its synthesis. It now starts to revolutionise, not merely its productive forces but its own categories, which now impossibly restrict those productive forces which its tension has generated. This movement is farther advanced in France, with Gide, Rolland, Malraux and Aragon wearing the uniform at which all once sneered. Here it has only begun ...

THE MOVEMENT OF BOURGEOIS POETRY

General Characteristics	*Technical Characteristics*

Primitive Accumulation, 1550–1600

The Elizabethan Age. – Marlowe, Shakespeare. The dynamic force of bourgeois individuality, realising itself by smashing all outward forms, is expressed in poetry. Its characteristic hero is the absolute prince, with his splendid public life, which is collective and through which other individualities can therefore realise themselves without negating his.

(a) The iambic rhythm, expressing the heroic nature of the bourgeois illusion in terms of the ancient world, is allowed to flower luxuriantly and naturally; it indicates the free and boundless development of the personal will. It is collective – adapted for declamation; noble – suitable to princely diction: flexible – because the whole life of the prince, even to its intimacies, is lived in easy openness.

(b) The lyrics are suitable for group singing (simple metres) but courtly (ornamental stanzas) and polished (bright conceits).

The Transition, 1600–1625

The Jacobean Age. – Donne, Herrick, Vaughan, Herbert, Crashaw. The absolute monarch now becomes a force producing corruption and there is a withdrawal from the brilliant public life of the court to the private study and the country.

The Puritan takes the lyric stanzas and makes them elaborate and scholarly. Court poetry becomes learned poetry with a study vocabulary. Blank verse (Webster) portrays the decline of princeliness and loses its noble undertone. The lyric is no longer singable and the conceits become knotted and thoughtful.

The Bourgeois Revolt, 1625–1650

The Puritan Revolution. – Milton. The bourgeoisie feels itself strong enough to revolt against the monarchy, and with the help of "the people", overthrows the Stuarts. But this realisation of bourgeois freedom proves dangerous: the people demand it too, and there is a dictatorship which isolates the bourgeoisie, followed by a reaction. The noble simplicity of the self-idealised revolutionary (Satan, Samson Agonistes, Christ in the desert) then vanishes in an atmosphere of defeat.

The heroic bourgeois illusion returns in terms of the ancient world but is more self-conscious and not projected into the figure of the prince. It is personal instead of dramatic. The puritan revolt against the court gives it a bare and learned vocabulary; and this conscious restraint is reflected in a stricter rhythm.

THE MOVEMENT OF BOURGEOIS POETRY

General Characteristics

Technical Characteristics

The Counter-Puritan Reaction, 1650–1688

The Restoration. – Dryden, Suckling, Lovelace. Poetry forgets its noble sentiments and becomes cynical, measured or rational. There is an alliance of the bourgeoisie with the aristocracy instead of the people; and the court returns, but no longer in the form of the absolute prince. The prince is now subject to "reason".

Formal rules are imposed to restrain the "spirit" whose violence has proved dangerous. Poetry indicates its readiness to compromise by moving within the bounds of the heroic couplet. Court poetry reappears for the bourgeoisie is allied with the aristocracy, and therefore the simple metres and courtly elegance of Elizabethan lyrics drive out the crabbed scholar's poems. The vocabulary becomes more conversational and social.

The Era of Mercantilism and Manufacture, 1688–1750

The Eighteenth Century. – Pope. The shortage of labour makes the bourgeoisie continue to ally itself with the agricultural capitalist (the Whig "aristocrat") in order to maintain the laws and restrictions which will keep down the price of labour and enable it to develop through the stage of manufacture. Poetry reflects a belief in the rightness and permanence of forms and restrictions, good taste and an upper-class "tone".

The outward "rules" are now accepted, not as a compromise but as obvious and rational ingredients of style. Poetry becomes Augustan, idealises style, measure, polish and the antithesis which restrains natural luxuriance. Vocabulary becomes formalised and elegantly fashionable.

THE MOVEMENT OF BOURGEOIS POETRY

General Characteristics

Technical Characteristics

The Industrial Revolution and the "Anti-Jacobin" Reaction, 1750–1825

The Romantic Revival. – Byron, Keats, Shelley and Wordsworth. The development from manufacture to machine power proletarianises the artisan class and makes the restrictions of mercantilism no longer necessary. The alliance between the landed capitalist and the petty bourgeois ends now that the expansion of the market and the development of machinery causes manufacture to fling off its subjection to the country and emerge as industry, the predominant force in the State. Small capitals now acquire huge expansive powers and the bourgeoisie grow light-headed with power. The forms of the era of manufacture are a check on industry. The "Liberal" capitalist leads the people in a crusade against privilege in the name of freedom. Poetry becomes ardent and full of feeling. It sees in itself a kinship to the Elizabethan era of individualism. It revolts against tradition and yearns for a fuller, freer life. But the alliance of the people with the bourgeoisie in the French Revolution leads to a revolutionary demand for proletarian freedom. The bourgeoisie becomes frightened, retracts its demands, loses its mass basis and enters on a reaction in alliance with the landed aristocracy. Poetry, disillusioned, more and more withdraws into the private world of romance. It is too compromised to make much of social reality except by extreme hypocrisy or empty pompousness. All poets now betray their youth as they mature.

Poetry revolts against the old "forms" by an appeal to the heart and the sentiments. Poetry demands simultaneously the inclusion of natural speech and the romanticising of speech by a return to Elizabethan and Jacobean metres and vocabularies. There is a strong injection of words expressing "abstract" ideas at the same time as sensuous and materially "rich" words come into vogue. Both combine to separate the poetic vocabulary from real life. Rhythm – with Elizabethan poetry declamatory, with Jacobean contemplative, with Puritan elevated, with Augustan elegant – becomes with Romantic poetry hypnotic. There is a great advance in the development of poetic technique.

THE MOVEMENT OF BOURGEOIS POETRY

General Characteristics	*Technical Characteristics*

The Decline of British Capitalism, 1825–1900

The Victorians. – Tennyson, Browning, Arnold, Swinburne, Rossetti, Patmore, Morris. The first capitalist crisis occurs in 1825. The poet becomes pessimistic or withdraws more and more into a private world, as the poet becomes isolated from society by the conditions of capitalist production.

A general intensification of the technical resources already discovered in the preceding era.

The Epoch of Imperialism, 1900–1930

"Art for Art's Sake"; the Parnassians; Symbolism; Futurism; Surréalisms. – The poet revolts by extreme individualism, commodity-fetishism and loss of control of social relations. The poem passes, by a series of stages, from the social world to the completely private world. This revolt against bourgeois conditions finally expresses in extreme purity the categories of bourgeois production. It thus negates itself in anarchy, and must necessarily move outside the bourgeois illusion. English poetry now follows behind the rest of Europe in its development, owing to the sheltered conditions of English capitalism. The classic example for development becomes French poetry and (secondarily) Italian, Spanish and Russian. Wilde, Eliot, Flecker and Pound may perhaps be mentioned. Victorian poetry persists in sheltered areas: the Country (Hardy, Thomas and Davies), Oxford and Cambridge (Housman, Brooke, Squire, etc.). The Great War expresses the insoluble antagonisms of developed capitalism, and the general economic crisis which follows it, 100 years after the first capitalistic crisis, closes this period.

The attempt entirely to separate the world of art from that of society. The rejection of all the specifically social features in poetry as a revolt against *convention*. Words increasingly used for personal associations. Either the rejection of all rhythm because of its social genesis or its use hypnotically to release associations which will be personal in proportion to their depth and therefore their unconsciousness. Finally, the "completely free" word of *surréalisme.*

THE MOVEMENT OF BOURGEOIS POETRY

General Characteristics

Technical Characteristics

The Final Capitalistic Crisis, 1930–?

The People's Front. – Poetry now expresses a real revolt against bourgeois conditions by an alliance of the bourgeois ideologist or "craftsman" with the proletariat against the bourgeoisie. France still leads: Aragon, Gide, etc. In England: Lewis, Auden and Spender.

An attempt once again to give a social value to all the technical resources, developed by the movement of the preceding stages. This period sees the beginning of a complete change of the whole content of poetry, which by the end of the preceding movement had become contentless and formal. The question of form now tends to take a second place until the problem of social relations has been solved poetically.

10

The World and the 'I'

* * *

Once again we must emphasise that neither the common perceptual world nor the common ego makes men think or feel in a standardised way. On the contrary, they are the very means whereby man realises his individual differences. To members of an animal species, the world looks very much alike because it is such a simple world: their lives cannot differ much within a narrow range. To a human being born in a highly civilised society, the world is so complex and elaborate that his life can be unique – completely realisable of his genetic individuality. In the same way, animals of one species must have a very similar emotional life: their emotional world is so simple. But the social ego has been so subtilised and refined by generations of art and experience, that an individual can realise his emotional peculiarities to the full within its frame.

A sunset is nothing to a beast; art makes it what it is to us. When words arouse a feeling-tone in us, we draw it from the social ego; otherwise how could a mere sound exactly arouse, like a note on a piano, a corresponding emotional reverberation selected from a socially recognised scale of values?

It is precisely because the complex social world and social ego offers such possibilities of realisation for the individuality, that we hear in modern civilisation so many complaints of the strangling of individuality by society. No such complaints are voiced in savage society, for the possibility of freedom does not yet exist. Man is too simple and cabined. When the development of the productive forces has been accomplished by a corresponding development in the social world and the social ego, giving man undreamed-of possibilities of self-realisation, and yet the *utilisation of these forces is manifestly held back by the productive relations*, then on all sides arise protests of 'emotional starvation' and 'crippling of personalities' in a world of rich consciousness, complaints which are the ideological counterpart of denunciations of malnutrition and unemployment in a world of plenty. They are part of the continually increasing volume of protest against modern society. They are the harbingers of revolution.

*　*　*

What then is the *purpose*, the social function, of science and art? Why are reared upon this mock world and this mock man a frigid but true image of reality and a phantastic but warm reflection of man's own countenance?

Both are generated as part of the social process: they are social products, and the social product whether material or ideological can have only one goal, that of freedom. It is freedom that man seeks in his struggle with Nature. This freedom, precisely because it cannot be won except by action, is not a freedom of mere contemplation. To attain it a man does not merely relapse into himself – 'let himself go'. Just as the spontaneity of art is the result of laborious action, so freedom has as its price, not eternal vigilance but eternal labour. Science and art are guides to action.

(1) *Science* makes available for the individual a deeper, more complex insight into outer reality. It modifies the perceptual content of his consciousness so that he can move about a world he more clearly and widely understands; and this penetration of reality extends beyond his dead environment to human beings considered objectively, that is, as objects of his *action*, as the anvil to his hammer. Because this enlarged and complex world is only opened up by men in association – being beyond the task of one man – it is a *social* reality, a world common to all men. Hence its enlargement permits the development of associated men to a higher plane at the same time as it extends the freedom of the individual. It is the consciousness of the necessity of outer reality.

(2) The other world of *art*, of organised emotion attached to experience, the world of the social ego that endures all and enjoys all and by its experience organises all, makes available for the individual a whole new universe of inner feeling and desire. It exposes the endless potentiality of the instincts and the 'heart' by revealing the various ways in which they may adapt themselves to experiences. It plays on the inner world of emotion as on a stringed instrument. It changes the emotional content of his consciousness so that he can react more subtly and deeply to the world. This penetration of inner reality, because it is achieved by men in association and has a complexity beyond the task of one man to achieve, also exposes the hearts of his fellow men and raises the whole communal feeling of society to a new plane of complexity. It makes possible new

levels of conscious sympathy, understanding and affection between men, matching the new levels of material organisation achieved by economic production. Just as in the rhythmic introversion of the tribal dance each performer retired into his heart, into the fountain of his instincts, to share in common with his fellows not a perceptual world but a world of instinct and blood-warm rhythm, so today the instinctive ego of art is the common man into which we retire to establish contact with our fellows. Art is the consciousness of the necessity of the instincts.

(3) It is important to understand that art is no more propaganda than science. That does not mean that neither has a social role to perform. On the contrary, their role is one which is as it were primary to and more fundamental than that of propaganda: that of changing men's minds.

They change men's minds in a special way. Take as an extreme case of science's way of changing man's view of outer reality, a mathematical demonstration. It cannot be said to persuade. A mathematical demonstration appears either true or false: if true, it simply injects itself into our minds as an additional piece of outer reality. If false, we reject it as mere word-spinning. But if we accept it, we are no more *persuaded* of its truth than we are persuaded of the 'truth' of a house standing in front of us. We do not accept it: we *see* it.

In the same way, in art, we are not persuaded of the existence of Hamlet's confusion or Prufrock's seedy world-weariness, we are not persuaded of the existence of Elsinore or Proust's madeleine cake. The whole feeling-complex of the poem or the play or the novel is injected into our subjective world. We *feel* so-and-so and such-and-such. We are no more persuaded of their truth than of the truth of a toothache: but the vividness or social universality of the emotional pattern is announced by the poignancy of the sensation we call Beauty. Music affords an even more striking example of this.

Thus neither Truth nor Beauty are persuasion, just because they are *guides* to action. Persuasion must be not a guide but a persuasion to action, a pressure to be or do differently. In fact science and art are opposite poles of language, and language has as its main function the role of *persuasion*. It has only evolved these poles as refinements, as tempered spear-heads of the advance of life. Art and science are persuasion become so specialised as to cease to be persuasion, just as in the flower petals the leaves have become so specialised as to cease to fulfil the function of leaves.

* * *

PART III

'Heredity and Development'

'Heredity and Development' was part of the collection of essays that Caudwell had prepared for publication when he went off to Spain. It takes the same fundamental Marxist position, which is elaborated in *Illusion and Reality* and *Studies in a Dying Culture*, that the economic structures in which people live shape the intellectual production of their society, but it has a somewhat different focus. It was not published with the other essays, for reasons which are advanced below. It seems appropriate to give it its own place in the volume.

The essay is concerned with science, an interest that runs through much of Caudwell's work, even the crime fiction. Concentrating on biology and genetics, his argument is that scientific theories, not just ideas that arise in everyday life, are shaped by the economic organisation of society. His unfinished *Crisis in Physics*, published in 1939, made the same argument, but obviously in a different subject.

Caudwell begins by pointing out that the important question for Darwin was not whether or not species changed – that change was widely recognised – but what was the mechanism of change: why and how did change occur? The bourgeoisie, Darwin's class, believed in progress through change and asserted that 'it could only come about through *free trade* – as a result of absence of social organisation, and by the free struggle of organism against organism under the pressure of natural needs. In other words, the progress of the bourgeoisie depended upon "natural selection".'[10] The theory not only reflected a class orientation but it also made it appear a principle of nature.

Caudwell then focused on the conflicting theories of what determines the individual's characteristics – genetic inheritance or environmental influence. This becomes one of his most interesting areas of philosophical discussion, the relation between subject and object. He argues with extensive illustration that environment and genetic inheritance cannot be meaningfully understood in isolation – they must be considered in their interaction. The explanations are more extended than the others in *Studies* and offer a brilliant example of dialectical reasoning.

The exclusion of 'Heredity and Development' from the *Studies* and *Further Studies* volumes was made with no notice and certainly no explanation. All but one of the other essays remaining after the publication of *Studies* were published in 1949 as *Further Studies in a Dying Culture* (Bodley Head). 'Romance and Realism', the other one left out in 1949, might have been considered too long for inclusion in the book (110 pages in the only edition, Princeton University Press, 1970) which may have been sufficient reason to exclude it. The length of 'Heredity and Development', however, is similar to that of the five essays of *Further Studies*. The reason for excluding it would seem to have been ideological and this surfaced in 1950–51 in the Communist Party theoretical journal, *The Modern Quarterly*, in short commentaries collectively known as the 'Caudwell Discussion'. Caudwell's dialectical view of genetics contradicted the official Soviet anti-genetics position based on the views of the agronomist Trofim Lysenko, who falsified research to 'prove' 'environmentally acquired inheritance'. With Stalin's backing, Lysenko's view became official Soviet policy and that of other Communist parties. Genetic science was eliminated in the Soviet Union and the policy retained its official status until some time after the death of Stalin. The editors of *Further Studies* chose not to challenge the party line. Aside from the treatment of the subject in 'Heredity and Development', Caudwell had indicated his dialectical view of genetics in a number of other places without extensive comment, but in this essay it was fully and explicitly expounded.

There are indications that Caudwell had some awareness of the conflict over genetics in the Soviet Union. But in the more explicitly political last chapter of *Illusion and Reality* he was critical of intellectuals who were willing to accept the discipline of the proletariat in all areas except that of their own professional expertise. He characterised the demand of scientists that scientific theory not be interfered with as the 'typically bourgeois conception of the scientist as a "lone wolf"'. Despite that gesture in *Illusion and Reality*, because his work was gaining a wide audience, there must have been pressure from the Communist Party leadership to discredit Caudwell's dialectical view of genetics. Hence the attacks in *Modern Quarterly*. One of his great strengths, his concrete explanation of Marxist principles, was labelled a distortion, and it was said scornfully that he appealed particularly to literary intellectuals by using the language of popular science. 'Heredity and Development' was finally published in 1986, in *Scenes and Actions: Unpublished Manuscripts*, edited by Jean Duparc and myself.

11

Heredity and Development: A Study of Bourgeois Biology

The work of Charles Darwin is rightly regarded as the most important event in the history of biology. It is compared to the work of Newton in the realm of physics. The law of evolution is felt to have acted as a unifying and elucidating principle throughout biology, in the same way as Newton's laws of motion and the law of gravity co-ordinated dynamics.

An important difference between the two men is that Newton's formulations were rapidly accepted, and were the basis of a continually expanding and interknit body of thought which endured unchallenged until the twentieth century. It was from the start a tightly argued and logically coherent structure. By contrast Darwin's theory was loose and contained logical flaws; it was opposed bitterly from the outset; and ever since it has given rise to much confusion in the minds of biologists about its most characteristic feature: the hypothesis of Natural Selection.

Darwin's theory had a double content. First of all it was a theory of evolution: the species were not fixed, but changed into one another with the course of time. The second was a theory of how this was accomplished: by natural selection. The first theory had been advanced in various forms before Darwin by a number of biologists, such as Erasmus Darwin, Buffon and Lamarck. The second theory was Darwin's own, but was invented almost simultaneously by Wallace. Until the discovery of the second part of his theory, Darwin held the first part to be of no value. It was only when as a result of his observation of fauna in the Galapagos Islands, and his acquaintance with the work of Malthus, he hit on this mechanism which could have produced evolution, that he felt that his theory ranked as a scientific hypothesis. He regarded this second part of the theory as a kind of confirmation or indispensable foundation, of a theory that animals changed by adapting themselves to their environment.

Yet in fact, while the first part of his theory of evolution lives on as the most vital content of biology, the second part has been repeatedly challenged and is now generally recognised to be formally incoherent. No biologist doubts that life changed and changes, as a result of its antagonistic relations with its surroundings. There is a body of evidence for this belief, such as morphological likenesses, the convergence and homology of organs, the linked series of fossils found in successive stratifications, and the re-enacting of tracts of ancestral history by the embryo and the larva. But this evidence is, as it were, a witness to the change, not to the cause of change, and the question ought to be asked whether a mechanism to produce all change in life was ever more than something tacked on to the theory of evolution. But this was far from being the opinion of Darwin and his followers. Natural selection was not something tacked on to evolution, but the pin on which the whole theory turned. Without it Darwin would have seen no meaning in a theory of evolution.

Science in its development has repeatedly thrown up and then thrown away scaffolding of this kind. For a long time accurate empirical data as to the 'flow' of heat and electricity were believed to depend on the theory of calorific and electric 'fluids' which were pictured as actually moving from one body to another. It is now realised that these data do not require such fluids. Heat is the motion of the molecules of matter: and electric current is the motion of the smaller particles of which molecules are composed. The old observations remain just as true, are in fact made subtler and more precise; but it is now seen that special fluids dwelling in matter are unnecessary. The observations depend on properties of matter under certain specific conditions.

In the same way, biology in the past attributed numbers of biological phenomena to an indwelling vital force, vital fluid, Archeus, or Spiritus Rector. These phenomena have since been explained as properties of matter, and the indwelling specific forces and mechanisms have been found to be unnecessary and tautologies rather than explanations. Yet such scaffoldings are not superfluous accidents. They are determined by the attitude to reality of the society which produces them.

The mechanism of Natural Selection is similar. The importance of the theory to Darwin's contemporaries, its hold on their imagination, the violence with which they defended it against the violent attacks of the 'older generation', suggest that the theory had a special attraction to the vanguard of that age.

When in fact we examine the theory of Natural Selection, we find that this machine for producing new species has a strange likeness to the capitalist economy of that era, as the capitalist saw it. Moreover the idea was suggested to Darwin by Malthus and the Galapagos Islands. Now Malthus is a bourgeois economist whose theory is based on the beliefs of his contemporaries about the proletariat; and in making his starting point 'conditions on an island', Darwin is following the example of all contemporary bourgeois economists. The political economy of Darwin's era, which produced Manchester liberalism and Free Trade was based on the following belief: If every man is left to himself to produce and exchange freely the commodities of society, the result will be for the maximum benefit of all, including himself. His private profit will be society's good. All exchange-value will then represent value to society, and just as much, and no more, will be produced than society needs, while every man will get a fair return for his labours. This political economy is justified by a consideration of what would happen if Robinson Crusoe produced for his own needs on a desert island and later a second Crusoe came on the scene.

Such a theory of economy reflects the programme of the bourgeois escaping from the feudal restraints upon trade. Above all, it expressed the 1750–1850 revolutionary upsurge of the new bourgeoisie against old aristocratic monopoly in capital and land. As long as England led the van in capitalist development, this revolutionary theory was the theory of 'free trade', as the result of which the most progressive country will automatically reap the lion's share of social profit. And just as 'free trade' in capitalist economy selected England, thereby proving her to be the country naturally the fittest, so natural selection in the world of nature assured a place in the vanguard for the fittest beasts.

This pleasant pastoral was the purest fairy tale. Unrestricted private property, unrestricted power to buy and sell products. necessarily arises from the capitalist economy of commodity production which goes through a historic development. Ownership of the means of production gives rise to capitalist profit – the exploitation of the labour-power of others. The resulting development of machinery produces the aggregation of capitals, the larger driving out the lesser. This involves the increase of fixed capital and a falling rate of profit, which produces 'crises' and desperate attempts to mitigate them, including the export of capital and the exploitation of colonies. Evolution proceeds, and gives rise to war. When the world is completely carved up, bourgeois free trade has become economic nationalism, the reign of tariffs, and the appearance of vast monopolies. Thus the peaceful equitable pastoral scene, simply by the development of the potentialities latent in it, has given rise to its lurid opposite. All is misery, monopoly, injustice, war.

Thus natural selection, in the sphere of economy, has not at all produced the kind of development one sees in the world of nature, but something peculiar, violent, and unprecedented. Natural selection is revealed by post-Darwinian history to be, not a natural law, but something peculiar to society, and not merely to society as a whole, but to capitalist society; and so unstable is it that it never exists except as an abstraction, in practice it is immediately unfolding its destructive negation.

Darwin came on the process half-way. The battle was already bitter, cruel and selfish, but capitalism was still on the upgrade, and this warfare of man against man was still increasing the productive forces of civilisation instead of (as to-day) throttling them. This bloody bourgeois struggle for existence was a progressive force, seen from the viewpoint of contemporary bourgeois man. A struggle for existence produces progress – this appeared to be the lesson of the time.

Darwin's youth was coloured by the incessant demand of the rising industrial bourgeoisie for always greater intensification of the struggle. The Corn Laws, which increased the cost of labour-power, were fetters on industrial production. They favoured a few – away with them therefore! This abrogation of 'protection' was repeated in all spheres. For this revolutionary class to which Darwin belonged, progress depended on the intensification of the individual struggle for existence, of course within the framework of bourgeois property rights. Natural selection then was a *class* theory.

The theory of *evolution* – the continual change of all that is – as opposed to the theory of evolution by natural selection, is not the distortion of ideology by a class struggle. To recognise evolution requires only that one has no vested interest in ignoring it and denying change. Change is so patent a fact of reality that it has been asserted in all ages, and only denied by the ideologists of a conservative ruling class which has outlived its functional usefulness, and is therefore concerned to assert all present categories as eternal. The industrial bourgeois of Darwin's time had no vested interest in denying change. On the contrary, it was to his interest to assert it, for he was by his actions rapidly changing the face of society. Those concerned with denying change were the vested interests of the

Church and the Tory landowners, whose privileges the bourgeoisie were attacking. From them therefore came the bitter opposition to Darwin.

On the other hand this bourgeois class, while it asserted change and asserted it as progressive and vital, asserted also that it could only come about through *free trade* – as a result of absence of social organisation, and by the free struggle of organism against organism under the pressure of natural needs. In other words, the progress of the bourgeoisie depended upon 'natural selection'.

The two parts of the Darwinian theory therefore expressed in the sphere of biology the complete bourgeois position at this time. It at once became more than a biological principle. It became the philosophy of the revolutionary bourgeoisie in all spheres of science. Newton's theories performed exactly the same function for the earlier bourgeois struggle here and on the Continent.

* * *

But the most remarkable assumption of the theory of natural selection is that the environment is solely inimical to the subject, and that the relations of members of a species is only that of deadly rivalry. For example, the herring is pictured as producing countless eggs, and the members of this progeny, by the competition for the limited food supply, wage a 'cold pogrom' against each other, which only a few can survive.

Such a conception of the relation of life as only inimical, both as among its members and as between life and the environment, is unfounded. For if the environment were only inimical to life, how could it be that life came into being and flourished out of the environment? And if members of a species are only in relations of mutual rivalry, how does a species emerge and solidify: should not this rivalry be a disruptive force in species?

In fact such a conception is simply the transference of capitalist society into nature. An earlier society saw Nature as a system, in which the whole world of life co-operated in mutual assistance. The herb fed the herbivore, the herbivore fed the carnivore, the carnivore was subject to man. Such a system was illusory as a complete explanation of the system of nature, because, although it pictured nature as a system of conscious relations, they were social and not natural relations. They saw the world as a vehicle of class relations, in which Will, as the willer imagines it to be, is the *type* of all relations. There is always a dominator whose will is free, and a dominated whose action is determined by the goal of the dominator. Such a view is a natural one for a feudal or slave-owning society, in which the domination of man over man is naked and unashamed; it becomes veiled in capitalist economy, where the capitalist's domination is veiled. In such a society the fundamental relation is not the naked and unashamed domination of man over man, but a disguised domination. It is secured by the Will's being regarded as free in its relations to property – i.e. to the environment. The struggles of the free wills for the sum of property appearing in the world markets, subject to the 'laws' of supply and demand, seem to secure the progress of society. For 'property', put 'food supply', for 'market', 'environment', for 'individual free will', 'individual struggle for existence', and for 'laws of supply and demand', 'physical laws', and there is a complete picture of the world of nature as seen by Darwin and his contemporaries. It is a self-consistent closed world, like the world of Newton. But it began to disintegrate almost at once as the result of experiment, whereas three centuries passed before Newton's closed world of physics cracked. Hence the extreme confusion of biology, a confusion which, just because it is now extreme and because biology was never thoroughly homogeneous, is not so startling to biologists as the splitting of the once monolithic closed world of physics is to physicists.

This world of biology, reflecting capitalist economy, not as it is but as the capitalist sees it, is almost as fictitious as the system of Nature of St. Thomas Aquinas or Aristotle. The same criticisms apply to it as to the capitalist's notions of his own economy.

* * *

The value of Darwinism therefore was that it persuaded men to see change in life, and see it as determined by the nature of matter. Such change can be seen in all periods where men's minds have not been frozen by the forms of a ruling class. The rapid increase in the productive forces of Darwin's era necessarily broke down the formulae of the conservative classes, and made men see the becoming of nature as never before. And just as the growth of capitalist economy was felt by capitalists as due to the pressure of the expanding market, so change in nature was seen as the pressure of the environment. Thus man for the first time conceived the world of nature as subject to impersonal laws.

The weakness of Darwinism was that it saw change through the ideology of a class society, an ideology necessarily one-sided therefore. The illusion of capitalism has two distorting effects on Darwinism.

(1) It pictures 'progress' or change as the result of an unrestricted struggle for profit (food), because this is how capitalism pictures its own economy. Looking below the surface, we can see that 'progress' and 'unrestricted struggle between organisms for existence' are far from being mutually dependent terms, but merely find themselves connected at a certain stage of social evolution. The unrestricted struggle leads ultimately to the decay of capitalism and to economic regression. It is not merely inadequate as a law of biological progress, but also as a law of capitalist progress.

(2) It sees life as insurgent against the dead environment. The environment or market poses of its unalterable nature certain problems, these life or the producer has to solve: this is the bourgeois conception of life's place in the scheme of nature. Such a conception is of course the reflex of the bourgeois attitude towards his social role: freedom consists in the unrestricted property right of the bourgeois over inanimate things which he manages for his profit by learning their laws. This is sufficient to give him freedom; and since every man is at liberty to acquire property to an unlimited extent, every man is capable of becoming free. Hence freedom appears to be a matter of knowing the market.

This conception is without justification in fact. A relation to a thing is a mutually determining relation, whether it be a relation of knowing or fabricating. In learning about or acting upon outer reality, man is himself altered, and this forms the basis for a new action. The market changes, not of itself, but by the action of men. A property right is not enough for freedom. The wills and actions of men make history certainly, but past history determines their wills and actions. Not only this, but the outcome of their joint wills, will not be the realisation of their individual wills, unless the co-operation of their willed actions (which produces history) is a *conscious* co-operation. But to accept this would involve the destruction of the whole picture of the bourgeois as a centre of free activity, securing progress by fulfilling his will without social restraint, against a background of the fixed, impersonal, environmental market.

Again, owing to the intimate interpenetration of environment and organism, a relation to property which is dominating and unrestricted necessarily becomes a dominating relation over men. All property (as distinct from unalienable natural traits) is social property. It is congealed labour; from its social role it derives its value and its being. It contains human life-blood – that of the men whose indispensable efforts produced it, and gave it its value. Bourgeois private property creates the exploited proletariat, and is the instrument of domination of the bourgeois class. History is made by their wills, but because they are unconscious of the determinism of society, including the determinism of their wills, their wills produce society's history blindly. There is a discrepancy between their conscious individual goals and the collective result of their actions. They bring about by their actions the opposite of what they will. The actions of the slave-owners first impoverished and then disrupted the Roman Empire, and the actions of capitalists to-day produce unemployment, war, and general decay.

The evolution of living objects is not therefore a case of life surmounting a certain set of obstacles posed by the environment, or the environment acting as a sieve to catch the higher elements in life's variations. The environment is not just property to be administered by the bourgeoisie, or a market whose fixed laws of supply and demand evoke the 'best results' from the living producer. The relation between them is mutually determining and developing. If we picture life diagrammatically as a series of steps, then at each step the environment has become different – there are different problems, different laws, different obstacles at each step, even though any series of steps beside its differences has certain general problems, laws and obstacles in common. Each new step of evolution is itself a new quality, and this involves a newness which affects both terms – organism and environment.

* * *

The contradictions inherent in the bourgeois view of life have given rise in the field of evolution to contradictions which, like other bourgeois dualisms, seem exclusive opposites but which when more deeply analysed prove to be merely different aspects of the fundamental bourgeois position. Of these perhaps the most familiar to biologists is the conflict between the neo-Darwinians and the neo-Lamarckians. This becomes a burning question in the form of the 'inheritance of acquired characters'. The neo-Darwinians deny the possibility of this; the neo-Lamarckians insist on its occurrence.

The neo-Darwinians hold that the evolution of species is the automatic result of the selecting process of the environment on the living organism. All adaptations are therefore 'chance' variations selected by chance.

The neo-Lamarckians, on the contrary, hold that the urges of the organism itself, in conflict with the environment, produce adaptations which are inherited. All adaptations are therefore purposive.

But the controversy is entirely without meaning in fact, because both schools separate the organism from the environment as exclusive opposites, of which one is living and changeful and the other inert and changeless. The two positions therefore correspond to the mechanical materialist and idealist positions in bourgeois metaphysics, and are generated by each other. If you separate the two in this absolute way, it is a matter of predisposition which view you adopt. If you are interested in the environment, and start from it as a basis, as the *real* thing, then all qualities (i.e. characters or adaptations) seem to be determined by the environment. If however you start from the organism, all adaptations will seem to be determined by the organism. Moreover, since you have separated the two, neither environment nor organism are real environment or real organism, for they are only *really* real as related parts of one real universe. Otherwise on the one hand there is a mechanical, unchanging environment, which therefore acts blindly and automatically, and on the other a free competitive organism, which therefore acts purposively with a desire undetermined by its environment – with unconscious, bourgeois free-will. These are both travesties of reality and cannot generate a causal explanation of life.

In the Darwinian explanation, this weakness is shown by a dependence on 'chance' variations – i.e. on variations of whose exact determinism we are ignorant. In the Lamarckian explanation, this weakness is shown by a dependence on spontaneous 'striving' – i.e. movement towards an undetermined goal. 'Spontaneity' is however simply the exclusively subjective aspect of that same ignorance of determinism of which 'chance' is the objective aspect.

In reality organism and environment are *both* contained in the *adaptation*, which is a subject-object relation. Hence the 'problem' of the transmission of acquired characteristics, which has rent biology and even driven a promising young biologist to fraud and suicide,[11] is in the way in which it is usually discussed, a problem without meaning.

The variations with which biology deals may be any quality from a colour to a habit. It is a new individual quality, by which this animal is differentiated from others of the species. It is then a new divergence from a type. Given in the recognition of a variation therefore is the existence of a species, a settled type from which there is variation, and the emergence of a new quality not before existent.

The question at issue between neo-Darwinians and neo-Lamarckians is: If the quality is acquired, can it be inherited? If a skin thickening, habit, longer horn or different tint is the result of something the animal 'does' when confronted with the 'problems' posed by the environment, will this character be shown in succeeding generations?

It is this question I call meaningless, for, in the distinction between acquired and innate characters, lies the same absolute distinction between organism and environment which leads always to a useless dualism and is the characteristic product of bourgeois culture.

A given quality of the animal can only manifest itself in a given environment or life-experience. For example, colours are dependent on certain chemicals in the food, mother love in hens demands a magnesium diet, and so on. For every specific quality, the environment must also be specified. Two strains of fowl will both be yellow-shanked fed on one kind of food; fed on another, one strain will be yellow and the other green-shanked. Is the green shank an acquired character? It is in fact impossible to distinguish between acquired and germinal characteristics, because all characters are germinal response to an acquired situation.

This arises from the fact that every organism has a life experience and is only known in that life experience. Its life experience is its environment. Its qualities represent a balance or synthesis between internal and external forces may produce a change in qualities, but only if the organism has the germinal aptitude for responding to that kind of external force in that kind of way. If pressure on the skin produces a callous, it can only do so because the skin is germinally such that it responds to pressure in that kind of way. A callous is an acquired character only in that sense. Mother love in hens is innate and hereditary, but if the diet is robbed of magnesium, the quality of mother love does not appear. Hence mother love is an acquired characteristic in the sense that it is acquired as the hen's reaction to magnesium.

* * *

Bourgeois science, by splitting itself up into biology, psychology, physics, aesthetics, etc., and then attempting to make each of these spheres self-contained at once raised insurmountable difficulties. By its very programme of closure it stated: 'Each of these spheres of qualities is in itself a material unity, but all together they are not a material unity.' This raised the problem of how these closed worlds, being self-determined, could all be known by man, for the knowability itself constituted a linkage between them, which was denied by the very method of the science. That is why, when physics reached a certain stage of development, epistemology (as expressed in Heisenberg's 'Principle of Indeterminacy') became the vital and basic problem. In biology this splitting raised the 'insoluble' problem of evolution – insoluble because environment and organism are artificially separated.

The theory of bourgeois science is not only split, it is static. It is based on bourgeois physics and therefore, on the eternity of 'property rights', the unchanging laws of the environment. Becoming physics first, and, making all changing qualities subjective, it gives a false picture of the environment as changeless. All it can give finally as reality is a circus of unchanging equations; yet even so, the 'instability' of these equations, indicating an unstable universe, produces a crisis in physics.

Bourgeois science now turns to living matter, in which it has piled up all reality's changing qualities, on the plea that they are subjective or 'living'. As a result it is faced in these spheres primarily with the task of explaining change by means of categories drawn from a changeless world. Biology (if we include psychology and sociology as departments) is simply the science of the change of qualities. Such qualities are relations between subject and object, but to bourgeois biology, because of the previous programme of physics, they are solely subjective or 'living qualities' – qualities of life. It followed from the very way the bourgeois tackled physics, that when he came to tackle 'biology', biology would simply be the science of changing quality. Evolution was therefore given in his programme from the start.

But since the world as seen by physics, excluding quality, had been rendered changeless, the change which is the feature of all reality (but which the bourgeois saw piled up solely in the sphere of life) came to him as a surprising novelty, a fact requiring explanation.

*　*　*

The bourgeois biologist wastes his time in seeking a general explanation for the change of living matter. The dialectical materialist seeks no such general explanation for a change in any part of reality, for change is what reality is. What the dialectical materialist seeks is the determining relations between the new qualities emerging in that change. Given in his task as a scientist is the establishment by theory and practice that all becoming is materially one. Therefore each new quality of change, as it emerges, must be determined by previous qualities, and his task is to uncover the hierarchy of such mutually determining relations.

The bourgeois biologist is so preoccupied with finding a reason for change as change, that he neglects to examine the structure of change. Science's task is not finding an explanation of change, any more than of finding an explanation for the existence of existents. Such a programme would be foolish. The bourgeois biologist as a Darwinian neglects this. He talks about 'chance variations'. This is like talking about unknowable data; science has no place for such language. It is precisely the determinism of variations with which science is concerned in evolution. Chance is a name for our ignorance of this. Yet the bourgeois biologist overlooks this, the real problem of biology, because he came to the study of life with an ideology that supposed change to be the activity of the free bourgeois, and that therefore the change of evolution was only explicable by a situation like that of capitalist economy. The same ideology had already introduced a dichotomy between organism and environment such that all definitions of 'characters' or 'adaptation', and of heredity or development, were made self-contradictory from the start.

Science however is not philosophy. In so far as it remains science and goes out in practice, it exposes its own contradictions. Thus the development of genetics, embryology and ecology has been the continual exposure of the errors in the bourgeois standpoint, and the continual transformation of leading concepts as a result. But since all such transformations are made within the circle of bourgeois categories, they produce, not the unification of the science but its disintegration into special studies, each of which represents a compromise between bourgeois metaphysics and a specific group of discoveries. Thus genetics and embryology have drifted apart, and genetics itself has split into a number of different studies. There is a limit to this kind of decomposition, and it already seems to be near. The synthesis cannot be brought about by a synthesis within biology, for it is just the posing of biology as a closed world separate from physics and sociology that is the root of the trouble. It can only be healed by the return to science of a common world-view.

Criticism of Darwinism is criticism of the contradictions that Darwinism unfolded within the circle of bourgeois categories. Darwinism as found in Darwin's writings is still fresh from contact with the multitude of new biological facts then being discovered. It does not as yet pose organism aridly against environment, but the web of life is still seen fluidly interpenetrating with the rest of reality. Germinal and acquired characteristics are distinguished as if they were separate things, but Darwin believes in the transmission of both. The extraordinary richness of the pageant of change, history and conflict in life which Darwin unfolds, gives an insurgent revolutionary power to his writings and those of such immediate followers as Huxley. Biology is still unified; but Darwinism already contained the contradictions which brought about its disintegration, and later biologists only developed them by the exposure of the whole system to the light of reality.

Of great importance in this connection was the work of Mendel, which was the negation of Darwin's theory of capitalist biology. Mendel was a priest, an Abbot of the order of Augustinian canons. He was opposed to all that industrial capitalism was doing in his world. His stand against the political innovations of developing capitalist economy in Germany, not only cut short his scientific work but ultimately worried him into an early grave.

He approached the study of variations therefore in a spirit opposed to change, resting on the eternal verities of logic and revelation; but he was also a scientist. He was devoted to the fact, to reality, to things as they are in practice. He was a scientist with a clerical viewpoint, just as Darwin was a scientist with a bourgeois viewpoint. And just as Darwin's bourgeois genius, as a result of his capitalist revolutionary ideology, looked for change and its causes, so Mendel's clerical genius looked for what must necessarily exist in change – the changeless, *that which* changes. Thus he discovered the Mendelian factors of heredity, whose assembly, beneath the changing mask of the phenotype, forms a predetermined genotype.

The fate of Mendel's ideas is proof that the ideology of an era is not the mere sum of the 'discoveries' of individuals, but that these discoveries receive their form and pressure from the social relations of the age. Mendel's discoveries were pressed out of existence until the twentieth century, when de Vries made similar discoveries and Mendel's forgotten work came to light.

Mendel's work was antagonistic to the concept of change for, taken as it stood, it showed that variations were not chance and spontaneous but predetermined. The factors were in themselves unchangeable; the apparent change of the phenotype arose from the masking of a recessive by a dominant character, a masking which only held with that particular individual. Behind the changing pageant of phenotypes an unchanging set of genes performed mathematical combinations.

Notes

1. C. St. John Sprigg, *"Let's Learn to Fly!"*. London: Thomas Nelson & Sons, 1937, p. 49. Subsequent citations will be given in parentheses (*LLF* + page number).
2. Neil Gore's lively play *Dare Devil Rides to Jarama* of 2016 deals with Clem Beckett's racing career and his partnership with Caudwell in the International Brigades defending the Spanish Republic against Franco's fascists. However, his caricature of Caudwell as an effete intellectual is rather unfair.
3. C. St. John Sprigg, *Crime in Kensington*. London: Eldon Press, 1933, p. 268.
4. Capt. H. D. Davis A.F.C. and Christopher Sprigg, *Fly with Me: An Elementary Textbook on the Art of Piloting*. London: John Hamilton, 1932, p. 14.
5. Christopher Caudwell, *Illusion and Reality: A Study of the Sources of Poetry*. London: Lawrence & Wishart, 1977 (first published, Macmillan, 1937), p. 18. Subsequent citations will be given in parentheses (*IR* + page number).
6. Karl Marx, *Contribution to The Critique of Political Economy*, in *Handbook of Marxism*, ed. Emile Burns. London: Martin Lawrence, 1935, pp. 371–2.
7. *Writing the Revolution: Cultural Criticism from Left Review*, ed. David Margolies. London: Pluto Press, 1998, p. 51.
8. Letter to Elizabeth Beard, 24 July 1935. This, and all other material from letters, is taken from *Christopher Caudwell, Scenes and Actions: Unpublished Manuscripts*, eds Jean Duparc and David Margolies. London: Routledge and Kegan Paul, 1986, p. 214. The collection of original unpublished material – letters, stories, theoretical work, etc. – is in the Harry Ransom Center of the University of Texas at Austin.
9. George Thomson, *Illusion and Reality*, Biographical note, 1946 edition.
10. 'Heredity and Development' in *Scenes and Actions*, p. 167.
11. I am grateful to Helena Sheehan for clarifying this. She believes the reference is to Paul Kammerer, an Austrian Lamarckist, who was working in the Soviet Union, was accused of fraud when he returned to Vienna, and then committed suicide. The USSR considered him a martyr of science.

Works Cited

AS CHRISTOPHER ST. JOHN SPRIGG

C. St. John Sprigg, *Crime in Kensington*. London: Eldon Press, 1933.

Capt. H. D. Davis A.F.C. and Christopher Sprigg, *Fly with Me: An Elementary Textbook on the Art of Piloting*. London: John Hamilton, 1932.

C. St. John Sprigg, *"Let's Learn to Fly!"*. London: Thomas Nelson & Sons, 1937.

AS CHRISTOPHER CAUDWELL

The Crisis in Physics, edited and introduced by Professor Hyman Levy. London: The Bodley Head, 1939.

Further Studies in a Dying Culture, edited with a preface by Edgell Rickword. London: The Bodley Head, 1949.

'Heredity and Development', in *Scenes and Actions*. See also Rob Wallace, 'Revolutionary Biology: The Dialectical Science of Christopher Caudwell', *Monthly Review* (November 2016).

Illusion and Reality: A Study of the Sources of Poetry. London: Lawrence and Wishart, 1977 (first edition, Macmillan, 1937).

Romance and Realism, edited and introduced by Samuel Hynes. Princeton, NJ: Princeton University Press, 1970.

Scenes and Action: Unpublished Manuscripts, edited and introduced by Jean Duparc and David Margolies. London: Routledge and Kegan Paul, 1986.

Studies in a Dying Culture, introduced by John Strachey. London: The Bodley Head, 1938.

This My Hand. London: Hamish Hamilton, 1936.

Index

The following terms are effectively *passim* and therefore are not indexed: Marx, Marxist, Marxian, bourgeois and, except where they are a focus of discussion, communism and fascism.